HEMINGWAY'S
PARIS

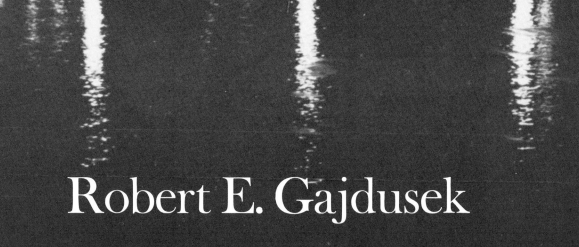

Robert E. Gajdusek

HEMINGWAY'S PARIS

CHARLES SCRIBNER'S SONS · NEW YORK

Copyright © 1978 Robert E. Gajdusek

Library of Congress Cataloging in Publication Data
Main entry under title:
Hemingway's Paris.
    1.   Hemingway, Ernest, 1899–1961—Homes and
haunts—France—Paris.   2.   Hemingway, Ernest,
1899–1961—Quotations.   3.   Authors, American—
20th century—Biography.   4.   Paris—Description—
Views.   I.   Hemingway, Ernest, 1899–1961.
II.   Gajdusek, Robert E.
PS3515.E37626   813'.5'2   78–17214
ISBN 0–684–17785–4

This book published simultaneously in the
United States of America and in Canada—
Copyright under the Berne Convention

1 3 5 7 9 11 13 15 17 19   Q/P   20 18 16 14 12 10 8 6 4 2

Permissions and acknowledgments appear on pp. 175–176.

Printed in the United States of America

Above: Chimney pots and rooftops seen from Hemingway's studio on rue Descartes.
Title page: The Seine.

Contents page: Hemingway, photographed in Paris in 1928.

Pages 8 and 9: View from Hemingway's studio on the rue Descartes.

Except for six passages by A. E. Hotchner this is a reprint of the clothbound
book published in 1978.

For my wife, Linda,
with whom I dine sumptuously
at the moveable feast

CONTENTS

INTRODUCTION

In 1918 Ernest Hemingway passed through Paris en route to the Italian front, where he served as an ambulance driver in the American Red Cross Field Service. He returned late in 1921, a recently married man of twenty-two, and with his wife, Hadley, settled into the city that was to become his home until 1928. Although his stay was soon interrupted by travels throughout Europe and the Near East—partly as foreign correspondent for the Toronto *Star*—and by a brief return to America, where his first son was born, Hemingway spent most of this period in Paris, "the town," as he once put it, "best organized for a writer to write in that there is."

Hemingway was passionately interested in the sights, scents, tastes, harmonies, and textures of the city and its people, and they provided stimulus for his work. In the mornings he usually wrote in a rented attic room on the rue Descartes, but he often worked in cafés as well. He was a voracious and discriminating reader of the books he borrowed from Shakespeare and Company or bought at the stalls on the quais. It was in Paris that he was befriended by James Joyce, Ezra Pound, Gertrude Stein, Ford Madox Ford, and F. Scott Fitzgerald, with whom he shared his early writings. There he wrote his first book of short stories, *In Our Time,* and his first published novel, *The Torrents of Spring.* There, too, he wrote most of *The Sun Also Rises* and began *A Farewell to Arms.*

His love affair with the city lasted throughout his life, and he returned to her many times after 1928. In 1944 he was a participant in the Allied liberation of Paris. While visiting again in 1949 he wrote most of the first draft of *Across the River and into the Trees,* and, after discovering his early manuscripts in the cellar of the Ritz, where they had been stored and forgotten, he conceived *A Moveable Feast,* an evocative memoir of Paris literary life.

This book takes a fresh look at Hemingway and his Paris. His own writings and those of his contemporaries, juxtaposed and reinforced with photographs, evoke the milieu and the man—judgment is left to the reader as the city emerges through image and word. Only a few of the photographs are drawn from archives. Most of them were taken recently, in order to show what of the past has persisted through an era of great change. Formal portraits of the writers have been excluded; their words suffice, heard against the landscape, and their true identities emerge from what they said and did.

The Paris of Hemingway's youth is considerably transformed. The ruins of Natalie Barney's temple *à l'Amitié* are almost concealed in an overgrown garden in the rue Jacob. Lavenue's, where expatriate writers often ate, is only a name carved on the walls above the Taverne de Maître Kanter. Michaud's, where Hemingway and Joyce often dined together, has been replaced by the Brasserie l'Escorailles. The Bal Musette, on the ground floor of Hemingway's first Paris home at 74, rue du Cardinal Lemoine, was turned into a pornographic movie house and, more recently, into an avant-garde theater. The attic room he rented on rue Descartes is being renovated—the skylight facing the Panthéon is gone, and there are plans to connect the room to the apartment beneath by a spiral staircase. All that remains of the sawmill apartment of 113, rue Notre-Dame-des-Champs are the cobblestones of the courtyard.

Yet there is survival, too. The Hôtel Jacob, today the Hôtel d'Angleterre, is still run by the same family. Shakespeare and Company, under new management and in a new location on rue de la Bûcherie near the quais, still holds part of Sylvia Beach's original collection and remains a meeting place for writers. The Dingo Bar on rue Delambre, where Hemingway and Fitzgerald first met, is now the Auberge du Centre, but you may still drink *fine à l'eau* at the original bar. Last year the Nègre de Toulouse became the Cahors, but its regional specialty remains *cassoulet.*

It is a pleasure to rediscover Hemingway's Paris and to find that so many of his favorite places still exist and still attract a large following. The Ritz and the Crillon, the Dôme, the Rotonde, the Select, the Deux Magots, the Flore, Lipp's, Prunier's, Harry's, the Hole in the Wall Bar—all serve new generations as they served the old. Some inconspicuous bars and cafés also capture a bygone age: the Falstaff Bar on rue Montparnasse, with its paneled walls and sifted afternoon light, and the very ordinary Caves Mura, a few blocks from the Opéra.

The market on rue Mouffetard still bustles with activity. The *clochards,* or hobos, still lie in the Place de la Contrescarpe. The girl who sits waiting in the Place St.-Michel is as beautiful as she has always been. The Seine pushes ceaselessly against the piers of the ancient bridges, and each spring the chestnut trees by the Closerie des Lilas unfurl their leaves above the raised sword of Marshal Ney's statue, while the waters in the fountain at the Place de l'Observatoire dash against the bronze horses. Paris is always Paris, and for Hemingway, who celebrated the eternal aspects of this changing earth, she was "the city I love best in all the world."

Robert E. Gajdusek, 1978

Note: Although a few minor corrections have been made for the sake of accuracy, the passages in this book have been reprinted verbatim. As a result, some variations in spelling, capitalization, punctuation, and the use of accent marks occur.

THE CITY

There is never any ending to Paris and the memory of each person who has lived in it differs from that of any other. We always returned to it no matter who we were or how it was changed or with what difficulties, or ease, it could be reached. Paris was always worth it and you received return for whatever you brought to it. But this is how Paris was in the early days when we were very poor and very happy.

Hemingway, *A Moveable Feast*, p. 211

"They say this Paris is quite a town, Papa. You ever been into it?"

"Yeah." . . . "The French call it *Paname* when they love it very much."

"I see," Archie said. *"Compris.* Just like something you might call a girl that wouldn't be her right name. Right?"

"Right." . . .

I couldn't say anything more then, because I had a funny choke in my throat and I had to clean my glasses because there now, below us, gray and always beautiful, was spread the city I love best in all the world.

Hemingway,
By-Line: Ernest Hemingway, p. 337

If you are lucky enough to have lived in Paris as a young man, then wherever you go for the rest of your life, it stays with you, for Paris is a moveable feast.

Hemingway, *A Moveable Feast*, title page

Paris is very beautiful this fall. It was a fine place to be quite young in and it is a necessary part of a man's education. We all loved it once and we lie if we say we didn't. But she is like a mistress who does not grow old and she has other lovers now. She was old to start with but we did not know it then. We thought she was just older than we were, and that was attractive then. So when we did not love her anymore we held it against her. But that was wrong because she is always the same age and she always has new lovers.

Hemingway,
By-Line: Ernest Hemingway, p. 136

Paris always remained his favorite city, and he finally got around to writing about the Paris he loved in the last years of his life. He was staying at the Ritz in the winter of 1956–57, when the baggagemen demanded that he claim two trunks that had been there since 1927, when he had moved from Paris. Mary Hemingway, who was with him, has written that when the trunks were opened he discovered the notebooks and papers of his early years. During the weeks that followed, he walked the streets of Paris, retracing the steps of his youth, and during the last few years of his life he lingered over those notebooks, collaborating with his younger self, walking around the Left Bank lost in memory, sitting in its cafés, re-creating conversations with people he knew then, reliving the experience of writing his early stories.

George Wickes, *Americans in Paris*, p. 167

AND THE ARTIST

Alexander Bridge. *Above:* Detail. *Below:* View across the bridge to Les Invalides.

The Seine, with the Louvre in the background.

Wintry treetops.

I would walk along the quais when I had finished work or when I was trying to think something out. It was easier to think if I was walking and doing something or seeing people doing something that they understood.

Hemingway, *A Moveable Feast*, p. 43

"I remember every bridge on the river from Suresnes to Charenton," Tommy told her.

"You can't."

"I can't name them. But I've got them in my head."

"I don't believe you can remember them all. And part of the river's ugly and many of the bridges are."

"I know it. But I was there a long time after I knew you, and papa and I used to walk the whole river. The ugly parts and the beautiful parts and I've fished a lot of it with different friends of mine."

"You really fished in the Seine?"

"Of course."

"Did papa fish it, too?"

"Not so much. He used to fish sometimes at Charenton. But he wanted to walk when he finished work and so we would walk until I got too tired and then get a bus back some way. After we had some money we used to take taxis or horsecabs."

Hemingway,
Islands in the Stream, pp. 188–89

You went down a stairway to the park and watched the fishermen there and under the great bridge. The good spots to fish changed with the height of the river and the fishermen used long, jointed, cane poles but fished with very fine leaders and light gear and quill floats and expertly baited the piece of water that they fished. They always caught some fish, and often they made excellent catches of the dace-like fish that were called *goujon*. They were delicious fried whole and I could eat a plateful. They were plump and sweet-fleshed with a finer flavor than fresh sardines even, and were not at all oily, and we ate them bones and all.

Hemingway, A Moveable Feast, p. 43

With the fishermen and the life on the river, the beautiful barges with their own life on board, the tugs with their smokestacks that folded back to pass under the bridges, pulling a tow of barges, the great elms on the stone banks of the river, the plane trees and in some places the poplars, I could never be lonely along the river.

Hemingway, A Moveable Feast, pp. 44–45

I knew several of the men who fished the fruitful parts of the Seine between the Ile St.-Louis and the Place du Vert Galant . . .

Travel writers wrote about the men fishing in the Seine as though they were crazy and never caught anything; but it was serious and productive fishing. Most of the fishermen were men who had small pensions, which they did not know then would become worthless with inflation, or keen fishermen who fished on their days or half-days off from work. There was better fishing at Charenton, where the Marne came into the Seine, and on either side of Paris, but there was very good fishing in Paris itself.

Hemingway, A Moveable Feast, p. 44

Fishermen along the Seine.

14

It is wonderful in Paris to stand on a bridge across the Seine looking up through the softly curtaining snow past the grey bulk of the Louvre, up the river spanned by many bridges and bordered by the grey houses of old Paris to where Notre Dame squats in the dusk.

It is very beautiful in Paris and very lonely at Christmas time.

Hemingway,
By-Line: Ernest Hemingway, p. 112

When we came back to Paris it was clear and cold and lovely. The city had accommodated itself to winter, there was good wood for sale at the wood and coal place across our street, and there were braziers outside of many of the good cafés so that you could keep warm on the terraces. Our own apartment was warm and cheerful. We burned *boulets* which were molded, egg-shaped lumps of coal dust, on the wood fire, and on the streets the winter light was beautiful.

Hemingway, *A Moveable Feast,* p. 11

With so many trees in the city, you could see the spring coming each day until a night of warm wind would bring it suddenly in one morning. Sometimes the heavy cold rains would beat it back so that it would seem that it would never come and that you were losing a season out of your life. This was the only truly sad time in Paris because it was unnatural. You expected to be sad in the fall. Part of you died each year when the leaves fell from the trees and their branches were bare against the wind and the cold, wintry light. But you knew there would always be the spring, as you knew the river would flow again after it was frozen. When the cold rains kept on and killed the spring, it was as though a young person had died for no reason.

In those days, though, the spring always came finally but it was frightening that it had nearly failed.

Hemingway, *A Moveable Feast,* p. 45

Hemingway, too, was back in Paris. I seldom passed St.-Germain-des-Prés that I did not see him either at the Café de Flore or Aux Deux Magots. Usually he was alone, bent over his notebook, writing slowly, as if he weighed every word, cutting his sentences sharply, as he chiseled his gem-hard prose. One had only to watch him take out a conical pencil sharpener, fit it carefully over his pencil, turn it slowly and methodically, and sweep the cedar shavings into his palm to know that he was a man intent on method and process. . . .

Although he still went without a hat or tie, his linen was clean, his shoes polished, his clothes well cut. He looked robust, prosperous, successful—a young man upon whom assurance sat like a horsehair plume upon the casque of a Garde Républicaine. Now and then Robert McAlmon, one of the most active of the expatriate editors and whose Contact Press had published Hemingway's first book, *Three Stories and Ten Poems,* would be at the table with him or Ford Madox Ford, a rotund English novelist and a professional gourmet and connoisseur of wines, who edited the *transatlantic review,* to which both Hemingway and Joyce contributed.

Sara Mayfield, *Exiles from Paradise,* pp. 135–36

To have come on all this new world of writing, with time to read in a city like Paris where there was a way of living well and working, no matter how poor you were, was like having a great treasure given to you.

Hemingway, *A Moveable Feast,* p. 134

The Seine with the Louvre in the background.

Above: Cherubs on the Alexander Bridge.
Above right: Gargoyles on Notre Dame.
Below right: Pruned trees at the Louvre.

19

Above: The Eiffel Tower and Parisian rooftops. *Right:* Two of Hemingway's favorite spots, the Café de Flore and Aux Deux Magots.

AUBERGE E

A LA BONNE
FRANQUETTE

CAFE

RUE
SAINT RUSTIQUE

22   *Above:* A restaurant off the Place du Tertre. *Right:* Two bars frequented by Hemingway, Le Trou dans le Mur and Harry's.

A table at the Nègre de Toulouse.

We ate well and cheaply and drank well and cheaply and slept well and warm together and loved each other.

Hemingway, *A Moveable Feast*, p. 51

You got very hungry when you did not eat enough in Paris because all the bakery shops had such good things in the windows and . . . you saw and smelled the food. . . .

. . . You could not go further toward the river without passing shops selling fruits, vegetables, wines, or bakery and pastry shops. But by choosing your way carefully . . . you did not pass too many places where things to eat were sold.

Hemingway, *A Moveable Feast*, pp. 69–70

"You're too thin, Hemingway," Sylvia [Beach] would say. "Are you eating enough?"

"Sure."

"What did you eat for lunch?"

My stomach would turn over and I would say, "I'm going home for lunch now."

"At three o'clock?"

"I didn't know it was that late."

Hemingway, *A Moveable Feast*, p. 70

It was a lovely spring day and I walked down from the Place de l'Observatoire through the little Luxembourg. The horse-chestnut trees were in blossom and there were many children playing on the graveled walks with their nurses sitting on the benches, and I saw wood pigeons in the trees and heard others that I could not see.

Hemingway, *A Moveable Feast*, p. 118

"I loved it in the fall," young Tom said. "We used to ride back home in a carriage, an open one, do you remember? Out of the Bois and then along the river with it just getting dark and the burning leaves smell and the tugs towing barges on the river."

Hemingway, *Islands in the Stream*, p. 188

A baker's cart filled with *baguettes*, long loaves of French bread.

Above: A fish market. *Below, left to right:* An artichoke stand, wine cases, a horsemeat market.

26

I went on up the street looking in the windows and happy with the spring evening and the people coming past. In the three principal cafés I saw people that I knew by sight and others that I knew to speak to. But there were always much nicer-looking people that I did not know that, in the evening with the lights just coming on, were hurrying to some place to drink together, to eat together and then to make love. The people in the principal cafés might do the same thing or they might just sit and drink and talk and love to be seen by others. The people that I liked and had not met went to the big cafés because they were lost in them and no one noticed them and they could be alone in them and be together. The big cafés were cheap then too, and all had good beer and the apéritifs cost reasonable prices that were clearly marked on the saucers that were served with them.

Hemingway, *A Moveable Feast*, pp. 99–100

Sitting at a café, one of the great pleasures of Paris.

The terrace of Le Cluny café.

[I] finally came out on the lee side of the Boulevard St.-Michel and worked on down it past the Cluny and the Boulevard St.-Germain until I came to a good café that I knew on the Place St.-Michel.

It was a pleasant café, warm and clean and friendly, and I hung up my old waterproof on the coat rack to dry and put my worn and weathered felt hat on the rack above the bench and ordered *café au lait*. . . .

A girl came in the café and sat by herself at a table near the window. . . .

I looked at her and she disturbed me and made me very excited. I wished I could put her in the story, or anywhere, but she had placed herself so she could watch the street and the entry and I knew she was waiting for someone. So I went on writing. . . .

I've seen you, beauty, and you belong to me now, whoever you are waiting for and if I never see you again, I thought. You belong to me and all Paris belongs to me and I belong to this notebook and this pencil.

Hemingway, *A Moveable Feast*, pp. 4–6

A girl in a café across from Notre Dame.

Overleaf: A wind-blown fountain in the Tuileries Gardens.

. . . and the winter winds blew across the surfaces of
the ponds and the fountains blew in the bright light.
Hemingway, *A Moveable Feast*, p. 11

. . . sometimes, if the day was bright, I would buy a liter of wine and a piece of bread and some sausage and sit in the sun and read one of the books I had bought and watch the fishing.

Hemingway, *A Moveable Feast*, p. 44

Reading beside the Seine.

It is Paris. It is a Paris bounded by the buyers' hotel, the Folies Bergere and the Olympia, traversed by the Grands Boulevards, monumented with Maxim's and the So-Different, and thickly blotched with the night life resorts of Montmartre. It is an artificial and feverish Paris operated at great profit for the entertainment of the buyer and his like who are willing to pay any prices for anything after a few drinks.

Hemingway,
The Star Weekly, Toronto, March 25, 1922,
or *The Wild Years*, p. 79

A culinary monument of Paris.

"One never sees the old figures nowadays," complained one of the old-timers. "The Quarter without Ernest Hemingway has lost something—he helped us to see it through his own eyes."

Sisley Huddleston, *Back to Montparnasse,* p. 278

He used to walk a great deal through the city, dressed simply in cap and worn jacket, looking like "a real son of the people,". . . He liked the simple people of Paris, the taxi drivers, the shopkeepers, the bartenders, the jockeys, the boxers, the ones he felt really knew what life was all about. If there was anything that Hemingway hated it was pretentiousness, and the French people have an unusual gift for deflating pomposity.

Alice Sokoloff,
Hadley: The First Mrs. Hemingway, p. 48

Paris was an awful big town after Milan. Seems like in Milan everybody is going somewhere and all the trams run somewhere and there ain't any sort of a mix-up, but Paris is all balled up and they never do straighten it out. I got to like it, though, part of it, anyway . . .

Hemingway, "My Old Man," p. 195

Boule players.

Overleaf: Paris rooftops.

DÉFENSE
d'AFFICHER
LIONEL HAMPTON
TRAVAILLEURS D
NETTOYAGE RATH
MONTSENY
sentant de la CNTF
AVRIL
ÉNÉGAL
URQUIE
JALITE
JUIN
Bd St-Germain 75005 Paris
Rue Madame 75006 Paris
répression
Mexique
s of Jaz
77 · 21H
quintet

"Have you been in Paris long? Do you like it here? You love Paris, do you not?"

"Who's she?" Georgette turned to me. "Do I have to talk to her?"

She turned to Frances, sitting smiling, her hands folded, her head poised on her long neck, her lips pursed ready to start talking again.

"No, I don't like Paris. It's expensive and dirty."

"Really? I find it so extraordinarily clean. One of the cleanest cities in all Europe."

"I find it dirty."

"How strange! But perhaps you have not been here very long."

"I've been here long enough."

"But it does have nice people in it. One must grant that."

Georgette turned to me. "You have nice friends."

Hemingway, *The Sun Also Rises,* pp. 18–19

That was the way Robert Cohn was about all of Paris. I wondered where Cohn got that incapacity to enjoy Paris. Possibly from Mencken. . . .

"I don't care for Paris."

So there you were. I was sorry for him, but it was not a thing you could do anything about . . .

Hemingway, *The Sun Also Rises,* pp. 42, 12

"What's the matter?" she asked. "Going on a party?"

"Sure. Aren't you?"

"I don't know. You never know in this town."

"Don't you like Paris?"

"No."

"Why don't you go somewhere else?"

"Isn't anywhere else."

Hemingway, *The Sun Also Rises,* pp. 14–15

It was spring in Paris and everything looked just a little too beautiful.

Hemingway, *By-Line: Ernest Hemingway,* p. 79

Opposite: "Post No Bills." *Above:* Buttresses of Notre Dame.

Overleaf. Left: The Eiffel Tower and statues in silhouette. *Right:* Ste.-Chapelle.

All of the sadness of the city came suddenly
with the first cold rains of winter, and there were no
more tops to the high white houses as you walked but
only the wet blackness of the street and the closed
doors of the small shops . . .

Hemingway, *A Moveable Feast,* p. 4

"Tell me something more about Paris because I love to think of you and Paris in the week."

"Daughter, why don't you lay off Paris?"

"But I've been in Paris, and I will go back there again, and I want to know. It is the loveliest city in the world, next to our own, and I want to know some things truly to take with me."

Hemingway, *Across the River and into the Trees*, p. 217

Left: Details of a corner on quai St.-Michel. *Below:* A scenic panel on a bakery window. *Opposite:* An art nouveau subway entrance.

46

All that in Paris. Ah, Paris. How far it was to Paris now. Paris in the morning. Paris in the evening. Paris at night. Paris in the morning again. Paris at noon, perhaps. Why not?

Hemingway, *The Torrents of Spring,* p. 75

But Paris was a very old city and we were young and nothing was simple there . . .

Hemingway, *A Moveable Feast,* p. 58

Below and right: Figures on the Alexander Bridge.

48

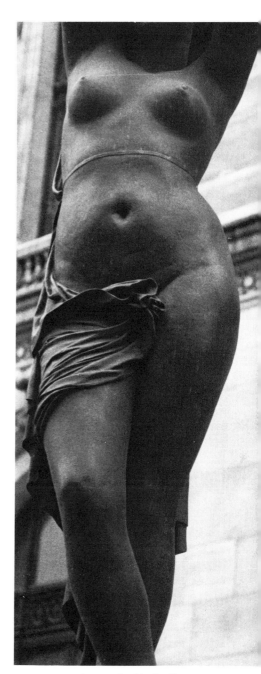

A statue beside the Opera.

The statue of a queen in the Luxembourg Gardens.

THE EARLY YEARS

This is to tell you about a young man named Ernest Hemmingway [*sic*], who lives in Paris, (an American) writes for the transatlantic Review & has a brilliant future. . . . I'd look him up right away. He's the real thing.

F. Scott Fitzgerald to Maxwell Perkins, in *Dear Scott/Dear Max,* p. 78

[Hemingway's] disappointment was softened by their arrival in Paris [in 1918] in the midst of the first shelling of the city by Big Bertha, the new, long-range German gun. At the Gare du Nord Hemingway gave Brumback his instructions. "Tell the taxi," he commanded his friend, "to drive up where those shells are falling. We'll get a story for the *Star* that'll make their eyes pop out back in Kansas City." A heavy tip to the driver allowed them to begin what Brumback recalled, with restraint, as "one of the strangest taxi drives I shall probably ever experience." They spent over an hour driving through Paris trying to catch up with the bursts. Finally they succeeded. "The shell hit the facade of the Madeleine," Brumback wrote, "chipping off a foot or so of stone." Perhaps by design, or perhaps merely by virtue of his own *Star* training, Brumback described the incident in 1936 in a facsimile of Hemingway's own prose. "No one was hurt. We heard the projectile rush overhead. It sounded as if it were going to land right in the taxi with us. It was quite exciting."

Charles A. Fenton, *The Apprenticeship of Ernest Hemingway,* p. 56

A statue of Danton.

Doorway of the Hôtel Jacob, now the Hôtel d'Angleterre.

Left: Le Pré aux Clercs restaurant.

Paris was wet and cold when they arrived there just a few days before Christmas [in 1921]. Sherwood Anderson had recommended the inexpensive, small Hotel Jacob, on the rue Jacob off the rue Bonaparte. It was clean but very simple and Hadley recalls the holes in the staircase carpet which Ernest referred to as "traps for drunken guests."

Alice Sokoloff,
Hadley: The First Mrs. Hemingway, p. 42

Lewis Galantière was a Chicagoan who worked for the International Chamber of Commerce. Elegant, energetic, and interested in all the arts, he hastened to invite the newcomers to dine with him at the Restaurant Michaud at the corner of rue Jacob and rue des Saints-Pères, near their hotel. It was a feast beyond their ordinary means, and by way of repaying the debt Ernest insisted that he and his host spar a bit in the hotel room. Galantière was soon winded, and put on his glasses. Still feinting and bobbing, Ernest broke them. But he was sorry, and helped pick up the pieces.

Alexander Winston, "If He Hadn't Been a Genius He Would Have Been a Cad," p. 29

. . . when they arrived in Paris [the] city was cold, damp, crowded, jolly, and beautiful. . . . [They] ate at the Pré aux Clercs in the rue Bonaparte. Dinner for two came to only twelve francs and good Pinard wine cost sixty centimes a bottle.

Carlos Baker, *Ernest Hemingway:
A Life Story,* p. 84

They started off Christmas morning strolling down the rue Bonaparte, along the Seine and across it, and the length of the Avenue de l'Opéra. By that time they had worked up an appetite. There was the Café de la Paix. They examined it judiciously and decided it looked the kind of place that would suit both the occasion and their limited budget. They had apéritifs and a fine meal that cheered them up even though it was unlike any Christmas dinner they had been accustomed to. Then the bill arrived. Later Hadley could not understand how they had missed adding up the prices of what they had ordered, but there it was. And they did not have enough money with them to pay the total. Ernest left a very nervous Hadley alone in the restaurant while he returned to the hotel for more money, running as fast as he could both ways.

Alice Sokoloff,
Hadley: The First Mrs. Hemingway, pp. 43–44

My old man had a big lot of money after that race and he took to coming into Paris oftener. If they raced at Tremblay he'd have them drop him in town on their way back to Maisons and he and I'd sit out in front of the Café de la Paix and watch the people go by. It's funny sitting there. There's streams of people going by and all sorts of guys come up and want to sell you things, and I loved to sit there with my old man.

Hemingway, "My Old Man," p. 200

Awnings of outdoor tables at the Café de la Paix.

Hemingway once lived in this building on rue du Cardinal Lemoine.

After the holidays, Lewis [Galantière] helped them find a place to live. It was a fourth-floor apartment at 74, rue du Cardinal Lemoine, a plebeian street that wound up from the Seine near Pont Sully and ended in a cobblestoned square called the Place de la Contrescarpe. Beside the front entrance at 74 was an angular building which housed a workmen's dance hall, or Bal Musette. Around the corner was the Café des Amateurs, "the cesspool of the rue Mouffetard," as Ernest called it, crowded with drunks and thick with smells.

Carlos Baker, *Ernest Hemingway: A Life Story,* p. 84

At every landing on the spiral staircase was a faucet and the ubiquitous French *pissoir.* The apartment was all funny angles and corners, and the furniture was "very elegant." In the bedroom was a great, gilt-trimmed fake mahogany bed, but the mattress was good, as it would be in France. The dining room was crowded with an ugly oak table and chairs. Both rooms served some of the functions of a living room. The bathroom consisted of a recessed closet with pitcher, bowl, and slop jar. Only one person at a time could get into the kitchen, with its two-burner gas stove. Slop jars had to be emptied at the landings and the garbage carried down the long four flights. The only heat was from a fireplace in the bedroom where they burned coal *boulets.* The other tenants were simple people, rough but kindly, all "salt of the earth with a little dark dirt mixed in." This was a poor working-class neighborhood.

Alice Sokoloff, *Hadley: The First Mrs. Hemingway,* p. 45

From the apartment you could only see the wood and coal man's place. He sold wine too, bad wine. The golden horse's head outside the Boucherie Chevaline where the carcasses hung yellow gold and red in the open window, and the green painted co-operative where they bought their wine; good wine and cheap. The rest was plaster walls and the windows of the neighbors. The neighbors who, at night, when some one lay drunk in the street, moaning and groaning in that typical French *ivresse* that you were propaganded to believe did not exist, would open their windows and then the murmur of talk.

Hemingway, "The Snows of Kilimanjaro," p. 70

As Ernest said, Ernest Hemingway said, in the early days—he came a little later than I—"You can live on less than less." A wonderful aphorism. Which was very true. Ernest and his first wife lived on less than less. There was something magnificent about Ernest's hospitality. They usually had an egg at lunch. So, if you were invited to lunch, you had an egg, too. There was always a glass of wine, usually some boiled potatoes. Ernest cared far less than I about aesthetics. What he cared about was the action and the emotional body of the traveler. He was a born traveler as he was a born novelist.

Janet Flanner to John Bainbridge, in *Another Way of Living,* p. 19

I had just come abroad and calling on Ezra Pound had asked him about American writers of talent then in Paris. Pound's answer was a taxi, which carried us with decrepit rapidity across the Left Bank, through the steep streets rising toward Mont Sainte Geneviève, and brought us to the rue du Cardinal Lemoine. There we climbed four flights of stairs to find Ernest Hemingway. . . . He was instinctively intelligent, disinterested, and not given to talking

Each landing in Hemingway's building had a faucet similar to this one.

nonsense. Toward his craft, he was humble, and had, moreover, the most complete literary integrity it has ever been my lot to encounter. I say the most complete, for while I have known others who were not to be corrupted, none of them was presented with the opportunities for corruption that assailed Hemingway. His was that innate and genial honesty which is the very chastity of talent; he knew that to be preserved it must constantly be protected. He could not be bought.

John Peale Bishop,
"Homage to Hemingway," p. 39

In the spring mornings I would work early while my wife still slept. The windows were open wide and the cobbles of the street were drying after the rain. The sun was drying the wet faces of the houses that faced the window. The shops were still shuttered. The goatherd came up the street blowing his pipes and a woman who lived on the floor above us came out onto the sidewalk with a big pot.

Hemingway, *A Moveable Feast*, p. 49

. . . and the cheap tall hotel [at 39, rue Descartes] where Paul Verlaine had died. There were only two rooms in the apartments where they lived and he had a room on the top floor of that hotel that cost him sixty francs a month where he did his writing, and from it he could see the roofs and chimney pots and all the hills of Paris.

Hemingway,
"The Snows of Kilimanjaro," p. 70

Here he spent long hours every day working to perfect his style, experimenting endlessly, searching for the ultimate in distillation and clarity.

Ernest was strict about his working hours. He and Hadley would have breakfast together, "but please, without speaking," and then he would be off to work in his room on the rue Mouffetard. Sometimes, when the work didn't go, he would trudge through the streets of Paris, observing, absorbing impressions and then go back again to wrestle at the Corona that Hadley had given him. She remembered that often when he came home after a long day

Hemingway's studio was on the top floor of this former hotel on rue Descartes.

there might be just one single line that he "could hang onto without hurting his conscience, his terrific artistic conscience."

Alice Sokoloff,
Hadley: The First Mrs. Hemingway, pp. 48–49

. . . the climb up to the top floor of the hotel where I worked, in a room that looked across all the roofs and the chimneys of the high hill of the quarter, was a pleasure. The fireplace drew well in the room and it was warm and pleasant to work. I brought mandarines and roasted chestnuts to the room in paper packets and peeled and ate the small tangerine-like oranges and threw their skins and spat their seeds in the fire when I ate them and roasted chestnuts when I was hungry. I was always hungry with the walking and the cold and the working. Up in the room I had a bottle of kirsch that we had brought back from the mountains and I took a drink of kirsch when I would get toward the end of the story or toward the end of the day's work. When I was through working for the day I put away the notebook, or the paper, in the drawer of the table and put any mandarines that were left in my pocket. They would freeze if they were left in the room at night.

Hemingway, *A Moveable Feast,* pp. 11–12

A view through the east window of the studio.

It was wonderful to walk down the long flights of stairs knowing that I'd had good luck working. I always worked until I had something done and I always stopped when I knew what was going to happen next. That way I could be sure of going on the next day. But sometimes when I was starting a new story and I could not get it going, I would sit in front of the fire and squeeze the peel of the little oranges into the edge of the flame and watch the sputter of blue that they made.

Hemingway, *A Moveable Feast,* p. 12

I would stand and look out over the roofs of Paris and think, "Do not worry. You have always written before and you will write now. All you have to do is write one true sentence. Write the truest sentence that you know." So finally I would write one true sentence, and then go on from there. It was easy then because there was always one true sentence that I knew or had seen or had heard someone say. If I started to write elaborately, or like someone introducing or presenting something, I found that I could cut that scrollwork or ornament out and throw it away and start with the first true simple declarative sentence I had written. Up in that room I decided that I would write one story about each thing that I knew about. I was trying to do this all the time I was writing, and it was good and severe discipline.

It was in that room too that I learned not to think about anything that I was writing from the time I stopped writing until I started again the next day. That way my subconscious would be working on it and at the same time I would be listening to other people and noticing everything, I hoped; learning, I hoped; and I would read so that I would not think about my work and make myself impotent to do it.

Hemingway, *A Moveable Feast,* pp. 12–13

58

... and I knew how much it would cost for a bundle of small twigs, three wire-wrapped packets of short, half-pencil length pieces of split pine to catch fire from the twigs, and then the bundle of half-dried lengths of hard wood that I must buy to make a fire that would warm the room.

Hemingway, *A Moveable Feast*, p. 4

Just down the street was the Place de la Contrescarpe, where the dregs from the rue Mouffetard would congregate in noisy bistros. Years earlier the *Place* had been the site of the celebrated Café de la Pomme de Pin where Villon and Rabelais used to visit, and Racine and La Fontaine, perhaps even Descartes, who had lived not far away on the rue Rollin.

Alice Sokoloff,
Hadley: The First Mrs. Hemingway, p. 46

You could dictate that, but you could not dictate the Place Contrescarpe where the flower sellers dyed their flowers in the street and the dye ran over the paving . . . and the old men and the women, always drunk on wine and bad marc; and the children with their noses running in the cold; the smell of dirty sweat and poverty and drunkenness at the Café des Amateurs and the whores at the Bal Musette they lived above.

Hemingway, "The Snows of Kilimanjaro," p. 69

. . . the rue Mouffetard, that wonderful narrow crowded market street which led into the Place Contrescarpe.

Hemingway, *A Moveable Feast*, p. 3

Opposite: Women shopping in the rue Mouffetard. *Top:* One form of Parisian fuel. *Bottom:* A wood and coal shop in Hemingway's neighborhood.

. . . where one could see tired beggars hoping for alms in front of the ancient church of Saint-Médard . . .

Alice Sokoloff,
Hadley: The First Mrs. Hemingway, p. 46

Around that *Place* there were two kinds; the drunkards and the sportifs. The drunkards killed their poverty that way; the sportifs took it out in exercise. . . . [In] that quarter across the street from a Boucherie Chevaline and a wine co-operative he had written the start of all he was to do. There never was another part of Paris that he loved like that, the sprawling trees, the old white plastered houses painted brown below, the long green of the auto-bus in that round square, . . . the sudden drop down the hill of the rue Cardinal Lemoine to the River, and the other way the narrow crowded world of the rue Mouffetard. The street that ran up toward the Pantheon and the other that he always took with the bicycle, the only asphalted street in all that quarter, smooth under the tires, with the high narrow houses . . .

Hemingway,
"The Snows of Kilimanjaro," pp. 69–70

Left: A *clochard* in the Place de la Contrescarpe. *Above:* Church of St.-Médard.

The *bal musette* (dance hall) next to the entrance of Hemingway's apartment building at 74, rue du Cardinal Lemoine, taken in 1975, the year it went out of business.

Next door to number 74 was a dance hall, a Bal Musette frequented by sailors and workingmen, a ten-cents-a-dance kind of place where you bought tokens for dances from the sharp-eyed manager. The slow shuffling of feet and the sound of the accordion were clearly audible in the Hemingways' apartment upstairs, playing them to sleep and often waking them up during the night.

Alice Sokoloff,
Hadley: The First Mrs. Hemingway, pp. 45–46

Sometimes the Hemingways went down to take a whirl. The place was dark and narrow, with wooden tables and benches along the walls, and a small bare space for dancing. . . . There was a scattering of sailors and *poules* among the customers. Patrons bought coins for each dance and anyone could dance with anyone else. . . . Hadley was occasionally frightened by the ruffians who asked her to dance. But Ernest seemed to revel in the smoky atmosphere. Spinning around the floor, wearing a striped Breton fisherman's shirt, he might have been mistaken for a native of the place.

Carlos Baker, *Ernest Hemingway:
A Life Story*, p. 95

. . . around the corner somewhere there is a little Bal Musette where the apaches . . . hang out with their girls, sit at long benches in the little smoky room, and dance to the music of a man with an accordion who keeps time with the stamping of his boots.

On gala nights there is a drummer at the Bal Musette, but the accordion player wears a string of bells around his ankle, and these, with the stamping of his boots as he sits swaying on a dais above the dancing floor, give the accent to the rhythm. The people that go to the Bal Musette do not need to have the artificial stimulant of the jazz band to force them to dance. They dance for the fun of it. . . .

Hemingway,
The Star Weekly, Toronto, March 25, 1922,
or *The Wild Years*, p. 80

After a while these parties grew so rough and so purposeless that Ford [Madox Ford], deciding he couldn't be responsible for such gatherings in his

Revelry at a dance hall.

own home, transferred them to a quiet little *bal musette* behind the Pantheon. . . .

Into this humble atmosphere Ford brought his gang. He took over the place one night a week and passed the word that his friends should come and make merry with him in the simple way of the older and gayer Paris. His *bal musette* salon did a thriving business for a while but it was not simple. All the characters out of *The Sun Also Rises* began to show

up, and there never was a night either that a taxi load of men from the rue du Louvre did not arrive about the time things got riotous in the Bucket of Blood, as the place came to be known. It could not continue. There came a night that was bound to be the last one. Ford announced that there would be no more soirées and the *bal musette* reverted to its former humble and respectable French uses.

Al Laney, *Paris Herald*, p. 163

The Louvre from the Tuileries.

L'Arc du Carrousel.

The Seine at night.

66

ONE OF ERNEST AND HADLEY'S WALKS IN PARIS

We walked back through the Tuileries . . . and stood and looked through the Arc du Carrousel up across the dark gardens with the lights of the Concorde behind the formal darkness and then the long rise of lights toward the Arc de Triomphe. Then we looked back toward the dark of the Louvre and I said, "Do you really think that the three arches are in line? These two and the Sermione in Milano?" . . .

Now we had come out of the gateway through the Louvre and crossed the street outside and were standing on the bridge leaning on the stone and looking down at the river. . . .

"We're watching the water now as it hits this buttress. Look what we can see when we look up the river."

We looked and there it all was: our river and our city and the island of our city.

"We're too lucky," she said. . . .

We walked across the bridge and were on our own side of the river. . . .

"Let's go to a wonderful place and have a truly grand dinner." . . .

So we walked up the rue des Saints-Pères to the corner of the rue Jacob stopping and looking in the windows at pictures and at furniture. We stood outside of Michaud's restaurant reading the posted menu. . . .

Standing there I wondered how much of what we had felt on the bridge was just hunger. I asked my wife and she said, "I don't know, Tatie. There are so many sorts of hunger. . . . Memory is hunger."

Hemingway, *A Moveable Feast*, pp. 53–57

An antique shop on rue des Saints-Pères.

When he eventually wired her to come down to Lausanne, Hadley thought that Ernest would like to show [Lincoln] Steffens more of his work. So she rounded up all Ernest's manuscripts and packed them into her little overnight bag, in which she also put all the necessaries for her train trip. No one saw her off, as no one knew she was leaving. She reached the Gare de Lyon well in time for the train. A porter took her luggage to the compartment, placed her big bag up out of the way and left the overnight case, with all the manuscripts, where she could easily get to it. There was still lots of time and so she went out and walked up and down on the platform where she met several newspaper correspondents she knew who were going to the same conference. When she got back to her compartment she thought at first she was in the wrong one as the overnight case was nowhere to be seen. But it wasn't in any of the other compartments either and then she realized that it had been stolen.

Alice Sokoloff,
Hadley: The First Mrs. Hemingway, p. 59

There were always other ways of disposing of what the man a woman is married to writes including the loss of everything the husband had written and not yet published (original manuscript, type-written copy and carbons; each in its separate folder) through having a suitcase stolen in the Gare de Lyon in 1922. A man's wife was bringing the manuscript and carbons for him to work on during a Christmas Vacation from working for The Toronto Star, INS and Universal Service at the Lausanne conference. The suitcase was stolen while she went out to buy herself a bottle of Vittel water.

But you do not marry a woman for her ability to care for manuscripts and I truly felt sorrier for how awfully she felt than I did for the loss of everything I had written. She was a lovely and loyal woman with bad luck with manuscripts.

Hemingway, "Preface,"
A Hemingway Check List, Lee Samuels, ed., p. 6

Ernest had not been back in Paris more than a week when a cable from the *Star* ordered him to Con-

stantinople to cover the war between Greece and Turkey. . . .

. . . The taxi to the Gare de Lyon on the night of September 25th was driven by a drunken chauffeur who hurled Ernest's suitcase out of the cab with such exuberance that the Corona typewriter inside was useless to him all through the long trip south. . . .

When the train chuffed into the Gare de Lyon at half past six on the morning of October 21, he had been away for more than three weeks. He was covered with bug bites and his hair was so lousy that he had to have his head shaved.

Carlos Baker, *Ernest Hemingway:
A Life Story*, pp. 97, 99

Gare de Lyon.

Above: Gare de l'Est. *Below:* Bookstall opposite Notre Dame.

. . . when I got back to Paris I should have caught the first train from the Gare de l'Est that would take me down to Austria. But the girl I was in love with was in Paris then, and I did not take the first train, or the second or the third.

Hemingway, *A Moveable Feast*, p. 210

To keep my mind off writing sometimes after I had worked I would read writers who were writing then, such as Aldous Huxley, D. H. Lawrence or any who had books published that I could get from Sylvia Beach's library or find along the quais.

Hemingway, *A Moveable Feast*, p. 26

The statue of a snake charmer outside the Reptile House.

70

He walked vigorously along the quais and would approach the cafés with a suggestion of the jogger's trot. But he could also dawdle over the bookstalls . . .
Ishbel Ross, *The Expatriates*, p. 257

In the bookstalls along the quais you could sometimes find American books that had just been published for sale very cheap. The Tour D'Argent restaurant had a few rooms above the restaurant that they rented in those days, giving the people who lived there a discount in the restaurant, and if the people who lived there left any books behind there was a bookstall not far along the quai where the *valet de chambre* sold them and you could buy them from the proprietress for a very few francs.
Hemingway, *A Moveable Feast*, p. 41

After that bookstall near the Tour D'Argent there were no others that sold American and English books until the quai des Grands Augustins. There were several from there on to beyond the quai Voltaire that sold books they bought from employees of the left bank hotels and especially the Hotel Voltaire which had a wealthier clientele than most.
Hemingway, *A Moveable Feast*, p. 42

People were coming out of the door of the reptile house when I went up to it. It was placarded as being open from eleven to three o'clock. It was twelve o'clock when I tried to enter.

"Is the reptile house closed?" I asked.

"Fermé!" the guard said.

"Why is it closed at this hour?" I asked.

"Fermé!" shouted the guard.

"Can you tell when it will be open?" I queried, still polite.

The guard gave me a snarl and said nothing.

"Can you tell me when it will be open?" I asked again.

"What business is it of yours?" said the guard, and slammed the door.
Hemingway,
The Star Weekly, Toronto, April 15, 1922,
or *The Wild Years*, pp. 82–83

Above: The Tour d'Argent.
Below: Hôtel Quai Voltaire.
Right: Along the quais.

A statue of Henri IV.

At the head of the Ile de la Cité below the Pont Neuf where there was the statue of Henri Quatre, the island ended in a point like the sharp bow of a ship and there was a small park at the water's edge with fine chestnut trees, huge and spreading, and in the currents and back waters that the Seine made flowing past, there were excellent places to fish.

Hemingway, *A Moveable Feast,* p. 43

The western end of the Ile de la Cité seen from the Left Bank.

In those days there was no money to buy books. I borrowed books from the rental library of Shakespeare and Company, which was the library and bookstore of Sylvia Beach at 12 rue de l'Odéon. On a cold windswept street, this was a warm, cheerful place with a big stove in winter, tables and shelves of books, new books in the window, and photographs on the wall of famous writers both dead and living. The photographs all looked like snapshots and even the dead writers looked as though they had really been alive.

Hemingway, *A Moveable Feast*, p. 35

A customer we liked, one who gave us no trouble, was that young man you saw almost every morning over there in a corner at Shakespeare and Company, reading the magazines or Captain Marryat or some other book. This was Ernest Hemingway, who turned up in Paris, as I remember, late in 1921. My "best customer," he called himself, a title that no one disputed with him. Great was our esteem for a customer who was not only a regular visitor, but spent money on books, a trait very pleasing to the proprietor of a small book business. . . . What had happened to his leg? Well, he told me apologetically, like a boy confessing he had been in a scrap, he had got wounded in the knee, fighting in Italy. Would I care to see it? Of course I would. So business at Shakespeare and Company was suspended while he removed his shoe and sock, and showed me the dreadful scars covering his leg and foot. The knee was the worst hurt, but the foot seemed to have been badly injured, too, from a burst of shrapnel, he said. In the hospital, they had thought he was done for; there was even some question of administering the last sacraments. But this was changed, with his feeble consent, to baptism—"just in case they were right." . . . Wyndham Lewis succeeded in making [James] Joyce squirm. And his article on Hemingway entitled "The Dumb Ox," which the subject of it picked up in my bookshop, I regret to say, roused him to such anger that he punched the heads off three dozen tulips, a birthday gift. As a result, the vase upset its contents over the books, after which Hemingway sat down at my desk

and wrote a check payable to Sylvia Beach for a sum that covered the damage twice over. . . .

I remember [Archibald] MacLeish and Hemingway meeting at the bookshop to discuss a certain plan to rescue Hart Crane, who for some reason was in a predicament with the French police. . . . I was very much touched when T. S. Eliot came over from London to read at Shakespeare and Company. Ernest Hemingway for once made an exception to his rule against reading in public and consented to appear if Stephen Spender could be persuaded to join him. So we had a double reading, and a great sensation it made!

Sylvia Beach,
Shakespeare and Company,
pp. 77, 78, 83, 121, 211

There was still a lot of shooting going on in the rue de l'Odéon [in 1944], and we were getting tired of it, when one day a string of jeeps came up the street and stopped in front of my house. I heard a deep voice calling: "Sylvia!" and everybody in the street took up the cry of "Sylvia!"

"It's Hemingway! It's Hemingway!" cried Adrienne [Monnier]. I flew downstairs; we met with a crash; he picked me up and swung me around and kissed me while people on the street and in the windows cheered.

We went up to Adrienne's apartment and sat Hemingway down. He was in battle dress, grimy and bloody. A machine gun clanked on the floor. He asked Adrienne for a piece of soap, and she gave him her last cake.

He wanted to know if there was anything he could do for us. We asked him if he could do something about the Nazi snipers on the roof tops in our street, particularly on Adrienne's roof top. He got his company out of the jeeps and took them up to the roof. We heard firing for the last time in the rue de l'Odéon. Hemingway and his men came down again and rode off in their jeeps—"to liberate," according to Hemingway, "the cellar at the Ritz."

Sylvia Beach,
Shakespeare and Company, pp. 219–20

It was in Sylvia's shop that I saw Ernest Hemingway for the first and last time. If this sounds portentous now, it is only because of all that has happened since to make of him a tragic figure. Then he was still the *beau garçon* who loved blood sports, the black-haired, sunburned muscle boy of American literature; the war hero with scars to show for it: the unalloyed male who had licked Style to a standstill. He had exactly the right attitude toward words like "glory" and so on. . . .

Sylvia ran to him calling like a bird, both arms out; they embraced in a manly sort of way (quite a feat, sizes and sexes considered), then Sylvia turned to me with that ominous apostolic sweetness in her eyes. Still holding one of Hemingway's hands, she reached at arm's length for mine. "Katherine Anne Porter," she said, pronouncing the names in full, "this is Ernest Hemingway. . . . Ernest, this is Katherine Anne, and I want the two best modern American writers to know each other!" Our hands

Shakespeare and Company as it is today.

I had dropped into Sylvia's shop looking for something to read, just at early dark on a cold, rainy winter evening, maybe in 1934, I am not sure. We were standing under the light at the big round table piled up with books, talking; and I was just saying good-bye when the door burst open, and Hemingway, unmistakably Ernest, stood before us, looking just like the snapshots of him then being everywhere published—tall, bulky, broadfaced (his season of boyish slenderness was short), cropped black moustache, watchful eyes, all reassuringly there.

He wore a streaming old raincoat and a drenched floppy rain hat pulled over his eyebrows.

were never joined.

"Modern" was a talismanic word then, but this time the magic failed. At that instant the telephone rang in the back room, Sylvia flew to answer, calling back to us merrily, merrily, "Now you two just get acquainted and I'll be right back." Hemingway and I stood and gazed unwinkingly at each other with poker faces for all of ten seconds, in silence. Hemingway then turned in one wide swing and hurled himself into the rainy darkness as he had hurled himself out of it, and that was all.

Katherine Anne Porter,
"Paris: A Little Incident in the Rue de l'Odéon,"
pp. 54–55

The facade of 27, rue de Fleurus, where Gertrude Stein had a studio apartment.

. . . I would walk up through the gardens and stop in at the studio apartment where Gertrude Stein lived at 27 rue de Fleurus.

. . . we had loved the big studio with the great paintings. It was like one of the best rooms in the finest museum except there was a big fireplace and it was warm and comfortable and they gave you good things to eat and tea and natural distilled liqueurs made from purple plums, yellow plums or wild raspberries.

Hemingway, *A Moveable Feast,* pp. 13–14

One time when I gave the excuse for not having stopped in at 27 rue de Fleurus for some time that I did not know whether Miss Stein would be at home, she said, "But Hemingway, you have the run of the place. Don't you know that? I mean it truly. Come in any time . . ."

Hemingway, *A Moveable Feast,* p. 117

One afternoon Hemingway came to her house very excited about Ford Madox Ford and the *Review.* He told Gertrude Stein that Ford wanted something of hers for the next number and that he, Hemingway, wanted *The Making of Americans* to be serialized in it; he must have the first fifty pages at once. Gertrude Stein was of course quite overcome with excitement at the idea, but there was no copy of the manuscript except the one that Alice Toklas and she had bound. "That makes no difference," said Hemingway, "I will copy it." Whereupon Miss Toklas and he did copy the manuscript, and it was printed in the April number of *The Transatlantic Review.*

Nicholas Joost, *Ernest Hemingway and the Little Magazines: The Paris Years,* p. 79

One day Hemingway took Fitzgerald to call on Miss Stein at her studio in the rue de Fleurus, and Fitzgerald charmed and was charmed by the

The exterior of the Stein apartment in the courtyard of 27, rue de Fleurus.

. . . yes sure I have a weakness for Hemingway. After all he was the first of the young men to knock at my door and he did make Ford print the first piece of The Making of Americans.

Gertrude Stein, *The Autobiography of Alice B. Toklas,* p. 215

priestess of the arts with her beefsteak laugh and quick perceptions.

Andrew Turnbull, *Scott Fitzgerald,* p. 153

And then we heard that he [Hemingway] was back in Paris and telling a number of people how much he wanted to see her [Gertrude]. Don't you come home with Hemingway on your arm, I used to say when she went out for a walk. Sure enough one day she did come back bringing him with her.

Gertrude Stein, *The Autobiography of Alice B. Toklas*, p. 220

Gertrude Stein wouldn't box but she liked a good listener, . . . and Ernest came often in his leather coat and blue sailor sweater to sit at her feet. "Gertrude Stein and me are just like brothers," he confided to Sherwood Anderson.

Alexander Winston, "If He Hadn't Been a Genius He Would Have Been a Cad," p. 30

André Masson and the . . . American poet, Evan Shipman . . . had been dining and wining rather heartily with Hemingway in Paris one evening. *"Allons chez Gertrude,"* Hemingway proposed, when they had finished; and so they went off to visit the *grande dame* of the rue de Fleurus, who was having a little gathering of her devotees that evening.

As usual the circle of admirers sat about and were hushed, while Miss Stein, in all her imposing bulk, paced back and forth slowly delivering one of her characteristic monologues—when Hemingway's party came clattering noisily into the salon, then relaxed, or rather relapsed, together upon a divan. They had arrived late, had interrupted Miss Stein, and what was more they were plainly tight. She appeared affronted, but after a moment resumed her speech, walking up and down, while fixing those three red-faced young men with her cold blue eye. Hemingway or Shipman may have ventured some observation that was displeasing to the hostess. At length, she exclaimed with feeling: *"Vous êtes tous une génération fichue!"*

Miss Stein afterward related that an old automobile mechanic, who used to service her Ford car, had used the same phrase in referring to the troubles he had with young apprentice workers serving in his shop in those days. After their years of war they were ill-trained and wanting in manual skill as mechanics, and so he had damned them

as a "lost generation." So Miss Stein, finding Hemingway and his friends logy with wine, had applied the same reproach to them. Out of that chance remark, made in a moment of petulance, came the monumental misnomer of the Lost Generation.

Matthew Josephson, *Life Among the Surrealists*, pp. 8–9

Ezra Pound was always a good friend and he was always doing things for people. The studio where he lived with his wife Dorothy on the rue Notre-Dame-des-Champs was as poor as Gertrude Stein's studio was rich. It had very good light and was heated by a stove and it had paintings by Japanese artists that Ezra knew.

Hemingway, *A Moveable Feast*, p. 107

One day when [Wyndham] Lewis rang the bell at Pound's flat he got no answer so he opened the door himself: 'A splendidly built young man, stript to the waist, and with a torso of dazzling white, was standing not far from me. He was tall, handsome, and serene, and was repelling with his boxing gloves—I thought without undue exertion—a hectic assault of Ezra's. After a final swing at the dazzling solar plexus (parried effortlessly by the trousered statue) Pound fell back upon his settee. The young man was Hemingway.'

Noel Stock, *The Life of Ezra Pound*, p. 248

Pound was then living in the *pavillon,* or summer house, that stood in the courtyard of 70 *bis,* rue Notre-Dame-des-Champs, near the Luxembourg Gardens. A big young man with intent eyes and a toothbrush mustache was there when I arrived, and Pound introduced him as Ernest Hemingway; I said that I had heard about him. Hemingway gave a slow Mid-western grin. He was then working for the International News Service, but there were rumors that he had stories in manuscript and that Pound had spoken of them as being something new in American literature. He didn't talk about the stories that afternoon; he listened as if with his eyes while Pound discussed the literary world. Very soon he rose, made a date with Pound for tennis the following day and went out the door, walking on the balls of his feet like a boxer. Pound continued his monologue.

Malcolm Cowley, *Exile's Return,* p. 120

The Pounds had invited other guests for later in the day, Hemingway among them. While Hemingway shadowboxed in another room, Ford took Joyce aside and asked him to contribute something to the new *transatlantic review.* . . . Joyce said ironically that it was a pity Ford had not been in time to ask Proust for a contribution. 'I have been told,' he said, 'that a single sentence of Proust would fill a whole magazine.'

Richard Ellmann, *James Joyce,* p. 569

[Pound] was living at the Hôtel Elysée, 9 rue de Beaune, and found temporary lodgings for [Joyce] close by at 9 rue de l'Université in a private hotel, which pleased Joyce by reminding him of Dublin. He came to Paris to stay a week and remained for twenty years.

Richard Ellmann, *James Joyce,* p. 496

"We would go out to drink and Joyce would fall into a fight. He couldn't even see the man so he'd say: 'Deal with him, Hemingway! Deal with him!' "

Hemingway quoted in Richard Ellmann, *James Joyce,* p. 708

"He really enjoyed drinking, and those nights when I'd bring him home after a protracted drinking bout, his wife, Nora, would open the door and say, 'Well, here comes James Joyce the author, drunk again with Ernest Hemingway.' "

Hemingway quoted in A. E. Hotchner, *Papa Hemingway,* pp. 53–54

He paid the bill and came out with Joyce over his shoulder like a half-empty sack. At Joyce's flat in the rue Galilée, Ernest carried the great man upstairs. When he came down, mopping his brow, he was almost sober. "No keys," he said. "Had to kick in the door." And then later, "Poor devil. At least he forgot the pain in his eyes."

Carlos Baker, *Ernest Hemingway: A Life Story,* p. 258

When he first came to Paris, Joyce stayed at this address.

A spot visited occasionally by Hemingway.

". . . The last night Joyce and his wife came to dinner and we had a pheasant and a quarter of the chevreuil with the saddle and Joyce and I got drunk because we were off for Africa the next day. God, we had a night."

Hemingway, *Green Hills of Africa*, p. 195

The conversation moved on to Hemingway, and Joyce said, "We were with him just before he went to Africa. He promised us a living lion. Fortunately we escaped that. But we would like to have the book he has written. He's a good writer, Hemingway. He writes as he is. We like him. He's a big, powerful peasant, as strong as a buffalo. A sportsman. And

ready to live the life he writes about. He would never have written if his body had not allowed him to live it. But giants of his sort are truly modest; there is much more behind Hemingway's form than people know."

Richard Ellmann, *James Joyce,* p. 708

During the whole month of November the address of the editorial office given on the [*transatlantic*] *review* stationery is still "65 Bd. Arago," and the business address, "19 Rue d'Antin," that of Bird's Consolidated Press Association office.

Bernard J. Poli, *Ford Madox Ford and the Transatlantic Review*, p. 25

William Bird was a journalist who had founded the Consolidated Press Association in 1919 and had become its European manager in Paris in 1920, with an office at 19 rue d'Antin. His hobby was to print books, and he first used an old press in Roger Dévigne's shop, l'Encrier, quai d'Anjou, on the Ile Saint-Louis. When a nearby shop became vacant in the winter of 1921, Bird moved in and had a press of his own. The address was 29 quai d'Anjou. In the spring of 1922 he met Hemingway at the Genoa Economic Conference. . . . In 1924 Hemingway's *In Our Time* . . . came out under the imprint of Bird's press, the Three Mountains Press.

Bernard J. Poli, *Ford Madox Ford and the Transatlantic Review,* pp. 14–15

. . . We went down the stairs to the café on the ground floor. I had discovered that was the best way to get rid of friends. Once you had a drink all you had to say was: "Well, I've got to get back and get off some cables," and it was done. It is very important to discover graceful exits like that in the newspaper business, where it is such an important part of the ethics that you should never seem to be working. Anyway, we went down-stairs to the bar and had a whiskey and soda. Cohn looked at the bottles in bins around the wall. "This is a good place," he said.

"There's a lot of liquor," I agreed. . . .

"Well," I said, "I've got to go up-stairs and get off some cables."

"Do you really have to go?"

"Yes, I've got to get these cables off."

Hemingway, *The Sun Also Rises,* pp. 11–12

Bill Bird noticed with amusement that Ernest had given Jake Barnes one of Bird's own favorite tricks for getting rid of bothersome friends: you asked them to have a drink at the Caves Mura, and after a suitable interval excused yourself on the plea of having to work.

Carlos Baker, *Ernest Hemingway: A Life Story,* p. 179

Among his friends Ernest did not spare himself. He was having a drink with Bill Bird at the Caves Mura when he blurted out the news that he and Hadley were getting a divorce. When Bill asked him why, Ernest answered flatly: "Because I am a son of a bitch."

Carlos Baker, *Ernest Hemingway: A Life Story,* p. 178

Through Hemingway, [Robert] McAlmon met William Bird, who had started the Three Mountains Press. . . . A year later Pound became the editor, and about the same time McAlmon joined with Bird to publish Contact Editions, which included books printed at the Three Mountains Press. Bird found a small office for Ford Madox Ford to use while editing the *transatlantic review.* . . .

Some idea of the importance of this publishing house can be gained from McAlmon's volume of 1925 entitled *Contact Collection of Contemporary Writers.* A selection of "works in progress," its contributors were: Djuna Barnes, Bryer, Mary Butts, Norman Douglas, Havelock Ellis, Ford Madox Ford, Wallace Gould, Ernest Hemingway, Marsden Hartley, H.D., James Joyce, Mina Loy, Robert McAlmon, Ezra Pound, Dorothy Richardson, May Sinclair, Edith Sitwell, Gertrude Stein, and William Carlos Williams.

Ernest Earnest, *Expatriates and Patriots,* p. 257

The first time they met at Ezra's studio, Pound enthusiastically puffed Ernest to Ford; . . . said Ezra, "You ought to have had him for your subeditor. He's an experienced journalist. He writes very good verse and he's the finest prose stylist in the world. . . . He's disciplined, too."

Ford professed interest. Hemingway reminded him of an "Eton-Oxford, husky-ish young captain of a midland regiment of His Britannic Majesty." The arrangements were soon consummated.

Carlos Baker, *Ernest Hemingway: A Life Story,* p. 123

Like Gertrude Stein's studio or Sylvia Beach's Shakespeare and Company, Ford's office at 29 quai d'Anjou is one of the places in Paris where the renaissance of English prose began.

Bernard J. Poli, *Ford Madox Ford and the Transatlantic Review,* p. 165

"Ford asked me to read MSS for him," wrote Ernest, "and I used to go down there and take a batch of them out on the Quai and read them. . . . Some of the stories I used to rewrite for fun."

Carlos Baker, *Ernest Hemingway: A Life Story,* p. 123

Far left: Entrance to the building on the quai d'Anjou that housed the revolutionary Three Mountains Press. *Left:* Steps down to the quai opposite 29, quai d'Anjou. *Below:* A typical scene on the quai.

Hemingway said it was he who first found my work. His story was that one morning as he was about to go to the W.C., he picked up some mss. from Ford's desk, and he said he got so excited about my story, he forgot to button up his pants.

Nathan Asch quoted in Bernard J. Poli,
*Ford Madox Ford and
the Transatlantic Review,* p. 81

Hemingway really was much busier than Ford implied. Not only did he help with the editorial chores, he actually ran the *Review* for two issues while the editor was in America; he acted as a scout for Ford, securing some unlikely American contributors (his reporter friend Guy Hickok, Ring Lardner, and Donald Ogden Stewart) and some of his Parisian friends (Gertrude Stein, Ralph Cheever Dunning, and Evan Shipman) as well as the mad Baroness; and he contributed editorial matter, letters, and some of his best fiction.

Nicholas Joost, *Ernest Hemingway and
the Little Magazines: The Paris Years,* p. 74

With the end of the Saturday dancings, Ford resumed his Thursday afternoon teas. There could never have been "an artistic atmosphere younger or more pleasurable or more cordial than that which surrounded the *Review* offices and the Thursday teas when they were again instituted," for it was possible now to keep them intimate. . . . "On most Thursdays Mr. Hemingway shadow boxed at Mr. Bird's press, at the files of unsold reviews, and at my nose, shot tree-leopards that twined through the rails of the editorial gallery and told magnificent tales of the boundless prairies of his birth."

Ford Madox Ford quoted in Nicholas Joost,
*Ernest Hemingway and the Little Magazines:
The Paris Years,* pp. 73–74

Wearing worn tennis shoes and a patched jacket, Ernest appeared when he felt like it at Ford's Thursday literary teas in the Quai d'Anjou. It was there that he first met a well-dressed, dark-haired young man with broad shoulders, a firm chin, and the profile of a classical Greek wrestler. This was Harold Loeb, a Princeton alumnus eleven years out.

Carlos Baker, *Ernest Hemingway:
A Life Story,* p. 124

Hem was by this time a figure in the top valhalla of literary Paris. Ford Maddox Hueffer sought his help. . . . He was friends with Pound. He lunched with Joyce. He was taken up by Gertrude Stein. He was contemplating a book about bullfighting for Querschnitt which Picasso was to illustrate. . . . Hem was the cynosure of all eyes.

John Dos Passos, *The Best Times,* p. 154

Ezra founded something called Bel Esprit with Miss Natalie Barney who was a rich American woman and a patroness of the arts. Miss Barney had been a friend of Rémy de Gourmont who was before my time and she had a salon at her house on regular dates and a small Greek temple in her garden [at 20, rue Jacob]. Many American and French women with money enough had salons and I figured very early that they were excellent places for me to stay away from, but Miss Barney, I believe, was the only one that had a small Greek temple in her garden.

Ezra showed me the brochure for Bel Esprit and Miss Barney had allowed him to use the small Greek temple on the brochure. The idea of Bel Esprit was that we would all contribute a part of whatever we earned to provide a fund to get Mr. Eliot out of the bank so he would have money to write poetry. . . .

. . . Either you had Bel Esprit or you did not have it. If you had it you would subscribe to get the Major out of the bank. If you didn't it was too bad. Didn't they understand the significance of the small Greek temple? No? I thought so. Too bad, Mac. Keep your money. We wouldn't touch it. . . .

. . . The small Greek temple is, I believe, still in the garden. It was always a disappointment to me that we had not been able to get the Major out of the bank by Bel Esprit alone, as in my dreams I had pictured him as coming, perhaps, to live in the small Greek temple and that maybe I could go with

The temple *à l'Amitié* that Miss Natalie Barney, an American patroness of the arts, built in her garden on rue Jacob.

Ezra when we would drop in to crown him with laurel.

Hemingway, *A Moveable Feast,* pp. 110–12

I had dragged Hemingway along to a French literary afternoon where Gide and Jules Romains and others of that generation sat on stiff-backed chairs around a bookshop wall talking as though they had rehearsed all morning, but Hemingway, whom all of them were watching, watched the floor. It was too much for Gide. He dropped the topic, whatever it was, and drew Hemingway aside to explain how he punished his cat. He punished his cat, he said, by lifting him up by the scruff of his neck and saying PHT! in his face. Whether Hemingway restrained a desire to hit him, I don't know. I was watching the back of his head.

Archibald MacLeish,
A Continuing Journey, pp. 309–10

Given the habitual insularity of the expatriates, I was agreeably surprised one day when Hemingway told me that he would like to meet some French writers.

"Easiest thing in the world," I said to him. "I'll ask the secretary of the P.E.N. Club, of which I am a member, to invite you to their next dinner. I'll be there and introduce you to as many people as you wish." . . .

"We shall be happy to have your friend with us that evening," [the secretary] said to me. "But please tell him the occasion is informal, and that no speeches are to be delivered, except my very brief address as secretary of the organization. . . ."

I conveyed the message to Hemingway who seemed relieved to know that he would not have to dress up for the occasion.

"As for the speechifying part of it," he added, "you may assure [the secretary] that I wouldn't dream of making myself ridiculous by airing my rotten French in public."

Ernest was too modest about his French of which he had a fairly good if somewhat slangy knowledge.

The banquet in question was indeed international in scope. Apart from Hemingway, however, the only American writer who came was Gertrude Atherton. H. G. Wells, John Galsworthy, Thomas Mann, Paul Valéry, and Georges Duhamel were there, and the president of the club, of course, M. Jules Romains. . . .

. . . I glimpsed the athletic figure of Hemingway among a group of newcomers at the door. He said, "Hello," waved his hand, and edged toward me. He was in black tie and dinner coat. Perhaps, I thought, he has discovered that none of his "business" suits was presentable on an occasion such as this, however informal. But when he extricated himself from the group with which he had entered the room, I noticed with something approaching incredulous awe that his feet were encased in bright yellow shoes. "Well," I said to myself, "this may be his idea of informality," and I dismissed the matter from my mind. As Ernest began moving around among the guests who stood waiting for the signal to be seated at the long banquet table, however, I caught many a quizzical glance directed to the places where his lower extremities protruded from his black trousers. As they moved over the green carpet covering the floor, his shoes were two golden beetles scampering on a closely cropped lawn. Throughout this episode Ernest acted with perfect nonchalance.

As is generally the case in gatherings of this sort, the cuisine was utterly uninspired, the conversation even more so, and the atmosphere frigid with ennui. . . .

"Ernest," I asked, "how about meeting some of these French writers?"

Obviously he was in a bad mood. Something must have annoyed him during dinner.

"Why the hell should I meet any French writers?" he replied, and stomped out of the room.

Victor Llona, "The Sun Also Rose
for Ernest Hemingway," pp. 164–67

. . . I frequently passed Ernest Hemingway as I cut through the Luxembourg Gardens. He had put on flesh, grown a little moustache, and acquired a purplish scar on his forehead. His baggy tweed suit was patched at the elbows, and the pocket of his coat was torn from the notebooks jammed into it. With

Château du Luxembourg.

Luxembourg Gardens.

Leafless trees in the Luxembourg Gardens.

Bumby [Hemingway's son John Hadley, born in 1923] astride his hip and Hadley following him as silently as an Indian squaw, he strode along, his head down, kicking at the gravel with his sneakers.

     Sara Mayfield, *Exiles from Paradise,* pp. 107–8

By any standards we were still very poor and I still made such small economies as saying that I had been asked out for lunch and then spending two hours walking in the Luxembourg gardens and coming back to describe the marvelous lunch to my wife. When you are twenty-five and are a natural heavyweight, missing a meal makes you very hungry. But it also sharpens all of your perceptions . . .

     Hemingway, *A Moveable Feast,* pp. 100–101

. . . the best place to go was the Luxembourg gardens where you saw and smelled nothing to eat all the way from the Place de l'Observatoire to the rue de Vaugirard. There you could always go into the Luxembourg museum and all the paintings were sharpened and clearer and more beautiful if you were belly-empty, hollow-hungry.

     Hemingway, *A Moveable Feast,* p. 69

If I walked down by different streets to the Jardin du Luxembourg in the afternoon I could walk through the gardens and then go to the Musée du Luxembourg where the great paintings were that have now mostly been transferred to the Louvre and the Jeu de Paume. I went there nearly every day for the Cézannes and to see the Manets and the Monets

and the other Impressionists that I had first come to know about in the Art Institute at Chicago. I was learning something from the painting of Cézanne that made writing simple true sentences far from enough to make the stories have the dimensions that I was trying to put in them. I was learning very much from him but I was not articulate enough to explain it to anyone.

Hemingway, *A Moveable Feast,* p. 13

". . . I can remember the Jardin du Luxembourg well. I can remember afternoons with the boats on the lake by the fountain in the big garden with the trees. The paths through the trees were all gravelled and men played bowling games off to the left under the trees as we went down toward the Palace and there was a clock high up on the Palace. In the fall the leaves came down and I can remember the trees bare and the leaves on the gravel. I like to remember the fall best."

". . . The way everything smelled in the fall and the carnivals and the way the gravel was dry on top when everything was damp and the wind on the lake to sail the boats and the wind in the trees that brought the leaves down."

Hemingway, *Islands in the Stream,* p. 60

Now you were accustomed to see the bare trees against the sky and you walked on the fresh-washed gravel paths through the Luxembourg gardens in the clear sharp wind. The trees were sculpture without their leaves when you were reconciled to them . . .

Hemingway, *A Moveable Feast,* p. 11

Sailing a toy boat on the lake in the Luxembourg Gardens.

"Am also fond of the Jardin," Ernest said, "because it kept us from starvation. On days when the dinner pot was absolutely devoid of content, I would put Bumby, then about a year old, into the baby carriage and wheel him over here to the Jardin. There was always a *gendarme* on duty, but I knew that about four o'clock he would go to a bar across from the park to have a glass of wine. That's when I would appear with Mr. Bumby—and a pocketful of corn for the pigeons. I would sit on a bench, in my guise of buggy-pushing pigeon-lover, casing the flock for clarity of eye and plumpness. The Luxembourg was well known for the classiness of its pigeons. Once my selection was made, it was a simple matter to entice my victim with the corn, snatch him, wring his neck, and flip his carcass under Mr. Bumby's blanket. We got a little tired of pigeon that winter, but they filled many a void."

A. E. Hotchner, *Papa Hemingway,* p. 45

Right: A gendarme pensively striding through the Luxembourg Gardens; beyond him is the Panthéon. *Below:* Pigeons such as these were caught by Hemingway in the Luxembourg Gardens during one lean Paris winter.

"I can remember feeling the pigeons by me warm under the blanket when you killed them just before it was dark and how the feathers were smooth and I would stroke them and hold them close and keep my hands warm going home until the pigeons got cold too."

Hemingway, *Islands in the Stream,* p. 60

"Where did you kill the pigeons, papa?" David asked.

"Mostly down by the Medici Fountain just before they shut the gardens."

Hemingway, *Islands in the Stream,* p. 60

. . . and when they put up the bust of Flaubert in the Luxembourg on the short cut through the gardens on the way to the rue Soufflot *(one that we believed in, loved without criticism, heavy now in stone as an idol should be)*.

Hemingway, *Green Hills of Africa,* p. 71

A few days later I ran into Hemingway in the Luxembourg Gardens and he and I went to a café in the rue Guynemer for a brandy and soda. While we were sitting on the terrace an artist friend of Hemingway's came and sat with us; he told us the story of a man whose wife had left him on his wedding night. After he had left, Hemingway said, "That's curious. That's what happened to him. He is putting the story into the third person and torturing himself with it."

Burton Rascoe, *We Were Interrupted,* p. 187

One day, shortly after his return from Cuba where he had remained a long time, I spotted him coming out of the Luxembourg Gardens, and we talked. He fired questions at me. Where was everyone? The Dingo [Bar] looked deserted. He had been back in Paris nearly a week and a lot of the old faces were gone. Where, back to the States? he wanted to know. I told him it looked that way, and rattled off names of those who had gone back. A slow exodus. Dwindling American colony. The expatriate dream had begun to fade. How about me? Did I feel like going back? No, I told him, I still liked it here and always would. Then he threw me this thunderbolt out of the clear blue sky: "If you change your mind I'll pay your fare." He told me where he was staying. "Drop over tomorrow and I'll lend you the money." He playfully feinted a punch at my solar plexus, laughed, and walked off while I stood there stunned. . . . I was still in a kind of trance when I went to see

A statue of Flaubert.

him in his hotel room near the Café Flore next day. He wrote out a sizable check, handed it to me, and a week later, after saying goodbye to my *Tribune* friends I was on the boat.

Wambly Bald,
in *The Left Bank Revisited,* p. 289

. . . the park was closed so I had to walk down along it to the rue de Vaugirard and around the lower end of the park. It was sad when the park was closed and locked and I was sad walking around it instead of through it and in a hurry to get home to the rue Cardinal Lemoine. The day had started out so brightly too. I would have to work hard tomorrow. Work could cure almost anything, I believed then, and I believe now.

Hemingway, *A Moveable Feast,* p. 21

Overleaf: Chairs in the Luxembourg Gardens.

A gate into the Luxembourg Gardens on rue Guynemer.

The fountain in the Place de l'Observatoire.

. . . and how fine the fountains were at the Place de L'Observatoire *(water sheen rippling on the bronze of horses' manes, bronze breasts and shoulders, green under thin-flowing water)* . . .

Hemingway, *Green Hills of Africa,* pp. 70–71

"I'd wheel you across the street from the Closerie des Lilas and past the fountain with the bronze horses and the fish and the mermaids and down between the long *allées* of chestnut trees with the French children playing and their nurses on the benches beside the gravel paths—"

Hemingway, *Islands in the Stream,* p. 58

. . . the lad in the Rue de Notre Dame des Champs
At the carpenter's loft on the left-hand side going
  down—
The lad with the supple look like a sleepy panther—
And what became of him? Fame became of him.
Veteran out of the wars before he was twenty:
Famous at twenty-five: thirty a master—
Whittled a style for his time from a walnut stick
In a carpenter's loft in a street of that April city.

Archibald MacLeish from "Years of the Dog," *The Human Season,* p. 38

It was a pleasant street sloping down from the corner of the Avenue de l'Observatoire and the Boulevard du Montparnasse, an easy stroll from the Luxembourg Gardens, where Hadley could air the baby, a stone's throw from an unspoiled café called La Closerie des Lilas . . .

Carlos Baker, *Ernest Hemingway: A Life Story,* p. 122

Rue Notre-Dame-des-Champs.

... we had taken the upstairs of the pavilion in Notre Dame des Champs in the courtyard with the sawmill *(and the sudden whine of the saw, the smell of sawdust and the chestnut tree over the roof with a mad woman downstairs)* and the year worrying about money *(all of the stories back in the mail that came in through a slit in the saw-mill door, with notes of rejection that would never call them stories, but always anecdotes, sketches, contes, etc. They did not want them, and we lived on poireaux and drank cahors and water)* ...

Hemingway, *Green Hills of Africa,* p. 70

"We have the whole second story," Hadley recounted, "tiny kitchen, small dining room, toilet, small bedroom, medium sized sitting room with stove, dressing room where John Hadley sleeps and the linen and bath things are kept and a very comfortable bedroom."

Alice Sokoloff,
Hadley: The First Mrs. Hemingway, pp. 68–69

They lived, at the time, in an incredibly bare hovel, without a toilet or running water, and with a mattress spread on the floor for a bed; it was in the court of a lumberyard, on the second floor, to which one climbed by a flight of rickety steps. Hemingway's only income was from occasional newspaper dispatches for the North American Newspaper Alliance. The place in which they lived seemed utterly comfortless, but the Hemingways were well dressed and the baby's carriage was new and luxurious.

Burton Rascoe,
We Were Interrupted, pp. 186–87

... Ezra met us at our hotel and took us off to meet his friends. He led us through a narrow street and into a small square enclosing three trees and surrounded by narrow old wooden houses. Stopping outside one of these Ezra tilted his head and, looking up to a second floor window, shouted, 'Hem! ... Hem!' At these sounds a head with dark curly hair appeared over the wooden balcony outside the window and a voice said, 'Oh, it's you, Ezra! Come on up!'

At the top of the wooden steps to the Hemingway home there stood a very handsome young man in grey flannel trousers and a white pullover. Hemingway was still extremely slim and his clean-shaven face had a charming boyish quality. After introductions we were ushered into a small living-room where Mrs. Hemingway, a gentle young woman, was seated nursing a baby. Like so many young American couples, the Hemingways were most welcoming and attentive hosts and I was struck by the naturalness and modesty of the writer. When his baby became restive, he took it and tossed it in the air and tried to amuse it in the most endearing way.

Brigit Patmore,
My Friends When Young, p. 99

Went to Hemingway's at 10:30 to see the baby. Found him to be two pounds underweight, otherwise well. Retracted his foreskin. He naturally cried, to his parents' chagrin.

William Carlos Williams, *The Autobiography of William Carlos Williams,* p. 227

[Dos Passos] was always relieved to come back to see the Hemingways at the sawmill apartment, and even to assist in the ceremony of giving Bumby his evening bath.

He was on hand the day Ernest bought a large bright canvas called "The Farm" by a small dark Spaniard named Joan Miró. Evan Shipman had been coveting the picture and had persuaded Miró to sell it to him through a dealer. On learning that Ernest wanted to give it to Hadley as a present for her thirty-fourth birthday, Evan magnanimously offered to shoot dice for the right to buy it. Although Ernest won, the price of 5,000 francs was far more than he could afford. They all scurried around borrowing the money and triumphantly brought home the picture in a cab. Miró came to see it where it hung above the bed, content that it had fallen into such good hands.

Carlos Baker, *Ernest Hemingway: A Life Story,* p. 158

Cobblestones in the courtyard of 113, rue Notre-Dame-des-Champs, the only trace of the building that housed a sawmill and an apartment where the Hemingways lived.

Leeks, a staple of French cooking.

Some months earlier the Hemingways had met a girl from Arkansas named Pauline Pfeiffer, who worked for the Paris edition of *Vogue*. She had eyes that drooped, full sensual lips, a flat chest, short boyish hair and bird-like charm. Pauline thought it such a shame that Hadley lived in a hovel and wore clothes that Pauline would have tossed to the charwoman. At the Paris apartment she glimpsed Ernest in dirty socks, sprawled on the rumpled bed, his chin black with stubble. A brute, obviously; but the heart hath its order that the mind wots not of. Pauline wanted him . . .

Alexander Winston, "If He Hadn't Been a Genius He Would Have Been a Cad," p. 38

"What's *poireaux*?"
"Leeks."
"It looks like long, green, quite big onions," young Tom said. "Only it's not bright shiny like onions. It's dull shiny. The leaves are green and the ends are white. You boil it and eat it cold with olive oil and vinegar mixed with salt and pepper. You eat the whole thing, top and all. It's delicious. I believe I've eaten as much of it as maybe anyone in the world."

Hemingway, *Islands in the Stream*, p. 65

"They were pretty poor," Roger said. "I can remember when your father used to make up all young Tom's bottles in the morning and go to the market to buy the best and the cheapest vegetables. I'd meet him coming back from the market when I would be going out for breakfast."

"I was the finest judge of *poireaux* in the sixth arrondissement," Thomas Hudson told the boys.

Hemingway, *Islands in the Stream*, p. 65

Hadley quickly rehired the *femme de ménage*, Madame Henri Rohrbach, who had worked for her off and on before. Marie was a sturdy peasant from Mûr-de-Bretagne. She and her husband, who was called Ton-Ton, lived at 10 bis, Avenue des Gobelins. . . . She took at once to the child and often bore him away in a carriage . . . to see Ton-Ton. . . .

Carlos Baker, *Ernest Hemingway: A Life Story*, p. 123

He taught his friends among the *maquis* a fighting song which derived from his own life in Paris twenty-odd years earlier. It was one he had made his son John commit to memory as a child so that he could find his way home again:

Dix bis Avenue des Gobelins,
Dix BIS Avenue des GOBELINS,
DIX BIS AVENUE DES GOBELINS,
THAT'S WHERE MY BUMBY LIVES.

Although the *maquis* did not know its source, they accepted it happily as they moved in on occupied Paris.

Carlos Baker,
Hemingway and His Critics, pp. 6–7

10-*bis*, avenue des Gobelins, where the Hemingways' maid had an apartment.

By going through the back door of the bakery across the street *(left)*, and out the front door *(below)*, Hemingway took a shortcut to Boulevard Montparnasse.

102

It was a lovely evening and I had worked hard all day and left the flat over the sawmill and walked out through the courtyard with the stacked lumber, closed the door, crossed the street and went into the back door of the bakery that fronted on the Boulevard Montparnasse and out through the good bread smells of the ovens and the shop to the street. The lights were on in the bakery and outside it was the end of the day . . .

Hemingway, *A Moveable Feast,* p. 99

The Hemingways went for lunch almost every day to the Nègre de Toulouse, a restaurant where they felt very much at home and they grew to be good friends with all the personnel. Ernest would insist always that Hadley make the salad dressing, which she was sure was no better than what they would have been served, but she would do a lot of measuring with teaspoons and it became quite a ritual.

Alice Sokoloff,
Hadley: The First Mrs. Hemingway, p. 73

On the opposite side of the narrow rue Notre Dame des Champs, which was made up primarily of the backs of the shops on the Boulevard du Montparnasse, there was a door that opened onto a flight of stairs by which they could go down and then around and up into a bakery shop and out onto the Boulevard. Ernest knew that Hadley missed having a piano and he discovered that in the basement of the bakery was an old upright that they could rent. Hadley would freeze playing it, but at least she could work her fingers. . . .

Alice Sokoloff,
Hadley: The First Mrs. Hemingway, p. 71

. . . I walked in the early dusk up the street and stopped outside the terrace of the Nègre de Toulouse restaurant where our red and white checkered napkins were in the wooden napkin rings in the napkin rack waiting for us to come to dinner. I read the menu mimeographed in purple ink and saw that the *plat du jour* was cassoulet. It made me hungry to read the name.

Mr. Lavigne, the proprietor, asked me how my work had gone and I said it had gone very well. He said he had seen me working on the terrace of the Closerie des Lilas early in the morning but he had not spoken to me because I was so occupied.

Hemingway, *A Moveable Feast,* p. 99

The Hemingways frequently lunched at this neighborhood restaurant.

La Closerie des Lilas, the "nearest good" café to Hemingway's apartment on rue Notre-Dame-des-Champs.

By this time we were at the restaurant. I called to the *cocher* to stop. We got out and Georgette did not like the looks of the place. "This is no great thing of a restaurant."

"No," I said. "Maybe you would rather go to Foyot's. Why don't you keep the cab and go on?"

I had picked her up because of the vague sentimental idea that it would be nice to eat with some one. It was a long time since I had dined with a *poule*, and I had forgotten how dull it could be. We went into the restaurant, passed Madame Lavigne at the desk and into a little room. Georgette cheered up a little under the food.

"It isn't bad here," she said. "It isn't chic, but the food is all right."

Hemingway, *The Sun Also Rises*, p. 16

The night before [Harold Loeb and Bill Smith] left, Kitty Cannell gave them a farewell dinner at the Nègre de Toulouse. She invited Hadley and Ernest and they all walked to the restaurant. . . . She had been advising [Hemingway] to write stories with real plots in place of the *contes* which she felt were held together only by simple emotions. "Hey, Kit-

ty," said Ernest, "I'm taking your advice. I'm writing a novel full of plot and drama."

Carlos Baker, *Ernest Hemingway: A Life Story*, p. 154

[Hemingway wrote but never published] a little story about Ford and his wife Stella Bowen arguing petulantly over the wine at dinner one evening at the Nègre de Toulouse.

Carlos Baker, *Ernest Hemingway: A Life Story*, p. 128

The Closerie des Lilas was the nearest good café when we lived in the flat over the sawmill at 113 rue Notre-Dame-des-Champs, and it was one of the best cafés in Paris. It was warm inside in the winter and in the spring and fall it was very fine outside with the tables under the shade of the trees on the side where the statue of Marshal Ney was, and the square, regular tables under the big awnings along the boulevard.

Hemingway, *A Moveable Feast*, p. 81

"In some inexplicable way an accident."

Mary Hemingway

Oh, not inexplicable. Death explains,
that kind of death: rewinds remembrance
backward like a film track till the laughing man
among the lilacs, peeling the green stem,
waits for the gunshot where the play began;

rewinds those Africas and Idahos and Spains
to find the table at the Closerie des Lilas,
sticky with syrup, where the flash of joy
flamed into blackness like that flash of steel.

The gun between the teeth explains,
The shattered mouth foretells the singing boy.

Archibald MacLeish,
The Human Season, p. 42

But Archie [MacLeish] found him unwilling to talk esthetics. Their conversations at the Closerie des Lilas turned chiefly on boxing and baseball.

Carlos Baker, *Ernest Hemingway:
A Life Story,* p. 137

When in dead earnest, he would retreat to the Closerie des Lilas, and he wrote much of *The Sun Also Rises* over *café crème* at this quiet hideaway. With a horse chestnut and rabbit's foot in his pocket for luck, he hunched his broad shoulders over a marble-topped table and wrote and rewrote in blue French notebooks.

Ishbel Ross, *The Expatriates,* pp. 255–56

I sat in a corner with the afternoon light coming in over my shoulder and wrote in the notebook. The waiter brought me a *café crème* and I drank half of it when it cooled and left it on the table while I wrote. When I stopped writing I did not want to leave the river where I could see the trout in the pool, its surface pushing and swelling smooth against the re-sistance of the log-driven piles of the bridge. The story was about coming back from the war but there was no mention of the war in it.

Hemingway, *A Moveable Feast,* p. 76

Most of the clients were elderly bearded men in well-worn clothes who came with their wives or their mistresses and wore or did not wear thin red Legion of Honor ribbons in their lapels. We thought of them all hopefully as scientists or *savants* and they sat almost as long over an apéritif as the men in shabbier clothes who sat with their wives or mistresses over a *café crème* and wore the purple ribbon of the Palms of the Academy, which had nothing to do with the French Academy, and meant, we thought, that they were professors or instructors.

These people made it a comfortable café since they were all interested in each other and in their drinks or coffees, or infusions, and in the papers and periodicals which were fastened to rods, and no one was on exhibition.

Hemingway, *A Moveable Feast,* pp. 81–82

Hem and I would occasionally meet at the Closerie des Lilas at the corner of Saint-Michel and Montparnasse to drink some such innocuous fluid as vermouth cassis while we talked about the difficulties of putting things down on paper. We both were reading the Old Testament. We read to each other choice passages. The song of Deborah and Chronicles and Kings were our favorites. . . . My story was that basing his wiry short sentences on cablese and the King James Bible, Hem would become the first great American stylist.

It must have been in the spring because we sat out on the triangle of garden between the pavements of the two boulevards and I remember being amused by the fact that, in spite of its name, there was an actual lilac blooming in the Closerie.

John Dos Passos, *The Best Times,* pp. 141–42

Ernest was fond of [Ezra Pound] and regarded him as an excellent literary critic. They used to talk about writing at the Closerie des Lilas Café across from the old Bal Bullier dance hall.

Janet Flanner, *Paris Was Yesterday*, p. xvii

[Fitzgerald] had told me at the Closerie des Lilas how he wrote what he thought were good stories, and which really were good stories for the *Post*, and then changed them for submission, knowing exactly how he must make the twists that made them into salable magazine stories. I had been shocked at this and I said I thought it was whoring. He said it was whoring but that he had to do it as he made his money from the magazines to have money ahead to write decent books. I said that I did not believe anyone could write any way except the very best he could write without destroying his talent.

Hemingway, *A Moveable Feast*, pp. 155–56

"Joyce came here with me a few times," Ernest said. . . . "Miró and I were good friends; we were working hard but neither of us was selling anything. My stories would all come back with rejection slips and Miró's unsold canvases were piled up all over his studio. There was one that I had fallen in love with —a painting of his farm down south—it haunted me and even though I was broke I wanted to own it, but since we were such good friends, I insisted that we do it through a dealer. . . . The dealer made me sign a chattel mortgage so that if I defaulted on any payment, I would lose the painting and all money paid in. Well, I skimped and managed okay until the last payment. I hadn't sold any stories or articles and I didn't have a franc to my name. I asked the dealer for an extension but, of course, he preferred to keep my dough *and* the painting. That's where the Closerie comes in. The day the dough was due, I came in here sad-ass for a drink. The barman asked me what was wrong and I told him about the painting. He quietly passed the word around to the waiters and

they raised the money for me out of their own pockets."

A. E. Hotchner, *Papa Hemingway*, pp. 53–54

I passed Ney's statue standing among the new-leaved chestnut-trees in the arc-light. There was a faded purple wreath leaning against the base. I stopped and read the inscription: from the Bonapartist Groups, some date; I forget. He looked very fine, Marshal Ney in his top-boots, gesturing with his sword among the green new horse-chestnut leaves.

Hemingway, *The Sun Also Rises*, p. 29

Then as I was getting up to the Closerie des Lilas with the light on my old friend, the statue of Marshal Ney with his sword out and the shadows of the trees on the bronze, and he alone there and nobody behind him and what a fiasco he'd made of Waterloo, I thought that all generations were lost by something and always had been and always would be and I stopped at the Lilas to keep the statue company and drank a cold beer before going home to the flat over the sawmill. But sitting there with the beer, watching the statue and remembering how many days Ney had fought, personally, with the rear-guard on the retreat from Moscow that Napoleon had ridden away from in the coach with Caulaincourt, I thought of what a warm and affectionate friend Miss Stein had been and how beautifully she had spoken of Apollinaire and of his death on the day of the Armistice in 1918 with the crowd shouting *"à bas Guillaume"* and Apollinaire, in his delirium, thinking they were crying against him, and I thought, I will do my best to serve her and see she gets justice for the good work she has done as long as I can, so help me God and Mike Ney. But the hell with her lost-generation talk and all the dirty, easy labels.

Hemingway, *A Moveable Feast*, pp. 30–31

We . . . dined . . . with a succession of imaginary guests, shadowy, transitory offspring of our imaginations. Marshal Michel Ney, who commanded the rear guard in Napoleon's retreat from Russia (1812) and who also commanded Ernest's respect, was one guest.

"Didn't they behead you for some stupid reason?" I asked, hunting around in my head for a kernel of fact.

"No. They shot me," Ernest said, speaking for Ney. "They couldn't forgive me for supporting Bonaparte in the Hundred Days, or for my command at Waterloo."

"What did you do to keep up morale on that march from Moscow?"

"Morale? It is a term we did not use in the Emperor's army."

Mary Welsh Hemingway,
How It Was, p. 115

The statue of Marshal Ney near the Closerie des Lilas.

Notre Dame seen from downriver, "squatting against night sky."

THE SUN ALSO RISES

We went down-stairs and out onto the Boulevard St. Michel in the warm June evening.

"Where will we go?"

"Want to eat on the island?"

"Sure."

We walked down the Boulevard. At the juncture of the Rue Denfert-Rochereau with the Boulevard is a statue of two men in flowing robes. . . .

A taxi passed, some one in it waved, then banged for the driver to stop. The taxi backed up to the curb. In it was Brett.

"Beautiful lady," said Bill. "Going to kidnap us." . . .

"Come and have a drink . . ."

We got in the taxi. . . .

"We might as well go to the Closerie," Brett said. . . .

Sitting out on the terraces of the Lilas Brett ordered a whiskey and soda, I took one, too, and Bill took another pernod. . . .

Brett looked at me. "I was a fool to go away," she said. "One's an ass to leave Paris." . . .

"Is she really Lady something or other?" Bill asked in the taxi on our way down to the Ile Saint Louis. . . .

We ate dinner at Madame Lecomte's restaurant on the far side of the island. It was crowded with Americans and we had to stand up and wait for a place. Some one had put it in the American Women's Club list as a quaint restaurant on the Paris quais as yet untouched by Americans. . . .

We had a good meal, a roast chicken, new green beans, mashed potatoes, a salad, and some apple-pie and cheese. . . .

We walked along under the trees that grew out over the river on the Quai d'Orléans side of the island. Across the river were the broken walls of old houses that were being torn down. . . .

We walked on and circled the island. The river was dark and a bateau mouche went by, all bright with lights, going fast and quiet up and out of sight under the bridge. Down the river was Notre-Dame squatting against the night sky. We crossed to the left bank of the Seine by the wooden foot-bridge from the Quai de Bethune, and stopped on the bridge and looked down the river at Notre-Dame.

Restaurant Au Point Marie.

Standing on the bridge the island looked dark, the houses were high against the sky, and the trees were shadows.

"It's pretty grand," Bill said. "God, I love to get back."

We leaned on the wooden rail of the bridge and looked up the river to the lights of the big bridges. Below the water was smooth and black. It made no sound against the piles of the bridge. . . .

We crossed the bridge and walked up the Rue du Cardinal Lemoine. It was steep walking, and we went all the way up to the Place Contrescarpe. The arc-light shone through the leaves of the trees in the square, and underneath the trees was an S bus ready to start. Music came out of the door of the Negre Joyeux. . . .

We turned to the right off the Place Contrescarpe, walking along smooth narrow streets with high old houses on both sides. Some of the houses jutted out toward the street. Others were cut back. We came onto the Rue du Pot de Fer and followed it along until it brought us to the rigid north and south of the Rue Saint Jacques and then walked south, past Val de Grâce, set back behind the courtyard and the iron fence, to the Boulevard du Port Royal. . . .

We walked along Port Royal until it became Montparnasse, and then on past the Lilas, Lavigne's, and all the little cafés, Damoy's, crossed the street to the Rotonde, past its lights and tables to the Select.

Hemingway, *The Sun Also Rises,* pp. 72–78

MONTPARNASSE

Café du Dôme in the 1920s.

There are never any suicides in the quarter among
    people one knows
No successful suicides.
A Chinese boy kills himself and is dead.
(They continue to place his mail in the letter rack at
    the Dome)
A Norwegian boy kills himself and is dead.
(No one knows where the other Norwegian boy has
    gone)
They find a model dead
Alone in bed and very dead.
(It made almost unbearable trouble for the con-
    cierge)
Sweet oil, the white of eggs, mustard and water
    soapsuds and stomach pumps rescue the people
    one knows.
Every afternoon the people one knows can be found
    at the cafe.

Hemingway, *The Collected
Poems of Ernest Hemingway*, p. 23

In those days many people went to the cafés at the corner of the Boulevard Montparnasse and the Boulevard Raspail to be seen publicly and in a way such places anticipated the columnists as the daily substitutes for immortality.

Hemingway, *A Moveable Feast*, p. 81

The Dôme was crowded too, but there were people there who had worked.

    There were models who had worked and there were painters who had worked until the light was gone and there were writers who had finished a day's work for better or for worse, and there were drinkers and characters, some of whom I knew and some that were only decoration.

Hemingway, *A Moveable Feast*, p. 101

... those three cafés in Montparnasse, and the Dôme in particular, were something more than a paperback edition of the Ritz bar; they were the heart and nervous system of the American Literary Colony.

When young writers came to Paris for the first time, they dropped their luggage at a hotel on the Left Bank and went straight to the Dôme, in hope of meeting friends who had preceded them. Either they met the friends or else they made new ones. When they left for Brittany or the Mediterranean, in July, they went to the Dôme before their departure. A word dropped to acquaintances there was a more effective means of announcing their movements than a paragraph in the Paris edition of *The New York Herald.* The Dôme created and disseminated gossip. Americans went there to see who was having breakfast with whom, or had quarreled with whom, or was invited to sit at whose table; it was their living newspaper. . . .

Hemingway, who sometimes came to the Dôme for his morning coffee, was writing a new kind of very short stories and showed them to people in manuscript, or sometimes read them aloud. Some thought they were marvelous, some held their noses. There was a chaffering about those early stories that preceded the later bidding and bargaining among critics. . . .

One couldn't say that Hemingway was a leader among them, because he stood apart from the group, but the others were proud to be seen with him. It was an event of the evening if he passed the Dôme, tall, broad, and handsome, usually wearing a patched jacket and sneakers and often walking on the balls of his feet like a boxer. Arms waved in greeting from the sidewalk tables and friends ran out to urge him to sit down with them. "The occasions were charming little scenes, as if spontaneous even though repeated," says Nathan Asch in one of his unpub-

Le Dôme today, from the outside and . . .

The editors of little magazines went to the Dôme in search of contributors; it was easier than writing letters. Several American publishers went there to ask about young authors, for, in addition to its other functions, the Dôme was an over-the-table market that dealt in literary futures. I heard there in the early spring of 1923 that a young man named

lished books. "In view of the whole terrace, Hemingway would be striding toward the Montparnasse railroad station, his mind seemingly busy with the mechanics of someone's arrival or departure, and he wouldn't quite recognize whoever greeted him. Then suddenly his beautiful smile appeared that made those watching him also smile;

and with a will and an eagerness he put out his hands and warmly greeted his acquaintance, who, overcome by this reception, simply glowed; and who returned with Hem to the table as if with an overwhelming prize."

Malcolm Cowley,
A Second Flowering, pp. 57–60

A man used to come striding up to the Dôme about seven in the evening, sometimes alone, sometimes with his wife. "He wants to write but is short of funds," McAlmon explained, "so he's coaching a couple of American youngsters." . . . He talked incessantly about Spain and bulls but nobody took him very seriously until Adrienne [Monnier] said quietly one evening when we were predicting certain success for a writer whose name I do not now remember, "Hemingway will be the best known of you all." She spoke in French and some of the others did not understand her but I had great respect for her

scripts, to the last comma, would look on the printed page. . . . He never forgot the command of our generation to put down truth as we saw it and I see no reason now to disagree with Adrienne.

Bryer, *The Heart to Artemis,* pp. 212–14

Here's something [Nathan] Asch wrote about Hemingway: "Once in Paris he had a dinner-table argument with another young writer"—that was Nathan Asch—"about their respective talents. Later when they were walking toward the Dôme for coffee, Hemingway fell into a boxer's crouch and began feinting and jabbing. That was something he often did in those days. The other young writer began shadow boxing too. He hit Hemingway accidentally and Hemingway hit back, knocking him down. His mouth gritty, tasting bits of teeth, the other picked himself up and stumbled back to his hotel room. Later that night there was a knock at the

. . . from the inside.

critical judgment and asked her in some surprise why she felt that he was better than we were. "He cares," she said, "for his craft." (I imagine that she used the word *métier*) . . . After a hard day's work and some equally hard drinking, Hemingway went to a printer's shop in the late evening to learn how to set up type so as to know exactly how his manu-

door. It was Hemingway. 'I couldn't go to sleep until you forgave me,' he said. 'You know of course that I was wrong in the argument. You've got a lot of talent. You've got more of everything than any of us.' "

Malcolm Cowley quoted by Denis Brian,
in "The Importance of Knowing Ernest," p. 101

Statue of Balzac opposite the Dôme.

I had paused for a moment at the bar of the Dôme for an apéritif, and stood beside a tall slender woman who was also having something and who engaged me in conversation, at once informal and reserved. She had a rather long face, auburn hair, and wore an old green felt hat that came down over her eyes; moreover, she was dressed in tweeds and talked with an English accent. We were soon joined by a handsome but tired-looking Englishman whom she called "Mike," evidently her companion. They drank steadily, chatted with me, and then asked me to go along with them to Jimmy's Bar near the Place de l'Odéon, a place that had acquired some fame during my absence from France. In a relaxed way we carried on a light conversation, having three or four drinks and feeling ourselves all the more charming for that. Then Laurence Vail came into the bar and hailed the lady as "Duff." At this, I began to recall having heard about certain people in Paris who were supposed to be the models of Hemingway's "lost ones"; the very accent of their speech, the way they downed a drink ("Drink-up-cheerio"), and the bantering manner with its undertone of depression; it was all there.

Suddenly Harold Loeb himself strode in vigorously, saw Duff, and stood stock-still; he had evidently heard she was in town and gone looking for her. He sat down at our table and said little, but looked his feelings much as Robert Cohn was described as doing. Duff's English friend then made little signs of irritation at Harold's presence (quite as in the novel). Laurence Vail ventured the remark: "Well now, all we need is to have Ernest drop in to make it a quorum." Duff laughed that one off bravely, and took another drink. But Ernest did not come.

Matthew Josephson,
Life Among the Surrealists, pp. 320–21

116

AN EVENING IN PARIS FROM
THE SUN ALSO RISES

The dancing club was a *bal musette* in the Rue de la Montagne Sainte Geneviève. . . .

Outside in the street we looked for a taxi. . . .

I told the driver to go to the Parc Montsouris, and got in, and slammed the door. Brett was leaning back in the corner, her eyes closed. I got in and sat beside her. The cab started with a jerk.

"Oh, darling, I've been so miserable," Brett said.

The taxi went up the hill, passed the lighted square, then on into the dark, still climbing, then levelled out onto a dark street behind St. Etienne du Mont, went smoothly down the asphalt, passed the trees and the standing bus at the Place de la Contrescarpe, then turned onto the cobbles of the Rue Mouffetard. There were lighted bars and late open shops on each side of the street. We were sitting apart and we jolted close together going down the old street. Brett's hat was off. Her head was back. I saw her face in the lights from the open shops, then it was dark, then I saw her face clearly as we came out on the Avenue des Gobelins. The street was torn up and men were working on the car-tracks by the light of acetylene flares. Brett's face was white and the long line of her neck showed in the bright light of the flares. The street was dark again and I kissed her. . . .

We were sitting now like two strangers. On the right was the Parc Montsouris. The restaurant where they have the pool of live trout and where you can sit and look out over the park was closed and dark. . . .

"Café Select," I told the driver. "Boulevard Montparnasse." We drove straight down, turning around the Lion de Belfort that guards the passing Montrouge trams. Brett looked straight ahead. On the Boulevard Raspail, with the lights of Montparnasse in sight, Brett said: "Would you mind very much if I asked you to do something?"

"Don't be silly."

"Kiss me just once more before we get there."

Hemingway,
The Sun Also Rises, pp. 19–27

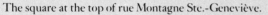

The square at the top of rue Montagne Ste.-Geneviève.

He had bought this pair of racing shoes second-hand from a waiter he knew at the Sélect who had been an Olympic champion and he had paid for them by painting a canvas of the proprietor the way the proprietor had wished to be painted.

"A little in the style of Manet, Monsieur Hudson. If you can do it."

It was not a Manet that Manet would have signed but it looked more like a Manet than it did like Hudson and it looked exactly like the proprietor. Thomas Hudson got the money for the bicycle shoes from it and for a long time they could have drinks on the house as well. Finally one night when he offered to pay for a drink, the offer was accepted and Thomas Hudson knew that payment on the portrait had been finished.

Hemingway, *Islands in the Stream,* p. 448

"Oh, I've just thought of something." She put her gloved hand up to her lips. "I know the real reason why Robert won't marry me, Jake. It's just come to me. They've sent it to me in a vision in the Café Select. Isn't it mystic? Some day they'll put a tablet up. Like at Lourdes. Do you want to hear, Robert? I'll tell you. It's so simple. I wonder why I never thought about it. Why, you see, Robert's always wanted to have a mistress, and if he doesn't marry me, why, then he's had one."

Hemingway, *The Sun Also Rises,* p. 51

The author of "A Farewell to Arms" is not irresistible to all women—to most, but not all. There was once one in Paris who refused to succumb.

No, she said, that would be too much to manage. I'm not going to give up a few years of my life to being in love with Hemingway.

So Hem would come to the Select every morning and push through the terrace chairs like a prowling animal with a wound.

Gee, have you seen ——— ——— about anywhere? he would ask, his eyes blank with pain.

Margaret Anderson,
My Thirty Years' War, p. 259

Miró was having dinner with the Hemingways, but after the boxing I told them I was meeting Loretto at the Sélect. And here again was the charm of Hemingway. I didn't have to say to him, "Loretto, I know, would like to meet Miró." He simply said, "We'll walk up with you." When we got to the café there was Loretto, and Hemingway introduced Miró and they sat down with us for a few minutes.

Morley Callaghan,
That Summer in Paris, p. 168

Hemingway felt that he was on top of the world during these days of inspiration in Paris. He was a productive, careful worker, and when he was busy he chose the cafés where he was least likely to be bothered by his fellows. He knew that the Sélect would mean chatter about horses and racing with Harold Stearns, and there was danger there, since he liked racing, gambling, tennis, and boxing. The revolutionaries liked the Rotonde, and the painters and writers who worked all day favored the Dôme, so Hemingway chose his bistros with forethought.

Ishbel Ross, *The Expatriates,* p. 255

The taxi stopped in front of the Rotonde. No matter what café in Montparnasse you ask a taxi-driver to bring you to from the right bank of the river, they always take you to the Rotonde. Ten years from now it will probably be the Dome. It was near enough anyway. I walked past the sad tables of the Rotonde to the Select.

Hemingway, *The Sun Also Rises,* p. 42

Le Select in the rain.

"American Bohemians in Paris a Weird Lot"
Paris, France.—The scum of Greenwich Village, New York, has been skimmed off and deposited in large ladlesful on that section of Paris adjacent to the Cafe Rotonde. New scum, of course, has risen to take the place of the old, but the oldest scum, the thickest scum and the scummiest scum has come across the ocean, somehow, and with its afternoon and evening levees has made the Rotonde the leading Latin Quarter show place for tourists in search of atmosphere.

It is a strange-acting and strange-looking breed that crowd the tables of the Cafe Rotonde. They have all striven so hard for a careless individuality of clothing that they have achieved a sort of uniformity of eccentricity. A first look into the smoky, high-ceilinged, table-crammed interior of the Rotonde gives the same feeling that hits you as you step into the bird house at the zoo. There seems to be a tremendous, raucous, many-pitched squawking going on broken up by many waiters who fly around through the smoke like so many black and white magpies. . . .

You can find anything you are looking for at the Rotonde—except serious artists. The trouble is that people who go on a tour of the Latin Quarter look in at the Rotonde and think they are seeing an assembly of the real artists of Paris. I want to correct that in a very public manner, for the artists of Paris who are turning out creditable work resent and loathe the Rotonde crowd. . . .

Hemingway,
By-Line: Ernest Hemingway, pp. 21–23

The tables are full—they are always full—someone is moved down and crowded together, something is knocked over, more people come in at the swinging door . . .

Hemingway,
By-Line: Ernest Hemingway, p. 21

. . . I persuaded a young newspaper man I knew to take me to the Rotonde. The terrace was so crowded with brass-bound, marble-topped tables that the Algerian rug peddlers and the purveyors of pornographic postcards had to walk in the gutter. Waiters in black coats and white aprons darted in and out like so many busy penguins among the noisy, bizarre-looking crowd of students, artists, models, and tourists. While we waited for one of them to find a seat for us, my friend nodded to a young man sitting

La Rotonde café.

alone reading a racing sheet in a corner against the partition that separated the Rotonde from the next café. "There's a chap that may do something someday," my friend said, pulling a clipping from his pocket. "He stayed with me at the Hotel Jacob when he first came here. A smart boy but a bit of a rough customer or we'd go sit with him."

The clipping he handed me was a feature story from the *Toronto Star Weekly,* "American Bohemians in Paris a Weird Lot," written, my friend told me, by the young man immersed in the racing sheet. . . . Even among the broad black hats and the flowing ties, the paint-smeared smocks and mandarin coats jammed together at the sidewalk tables, his clothes were conspicuously sloppy. He wore a dirty singlet, a pair of old corduroy trousers, grimy sneakers, and no hat. He was tall and well built but thin, almost gangling. His face was round, with high cheekbones, dimples, flat planes, and a deeply cleft chin. Had his skin not been so pale one might have suspected that he had Comanche blood. As it was, his sullen features, his dark hair, dark eyes, and long, dark sideburns made him look more like a Latin than an Indian. . . .

"If, as he says in his article, 'the artists of Paris who are turning out creditable work resent and loathe the Rotonde Crowd,' why does he come here?"

"To get away from the dump he lives in, I suppose. He gets his mail here, reads all the papers on the café rack, writes his stories at the table there—all for the price of a few demi-bocks." . . .

"[He] came to Paris to try to write. And unlike most of the literary crowd that hang out here, Hemingway's serious about it. Damn serious. . . . He showed me a story once that he'd rewritten eleven times and still hadn't finished it."

Sara Mayfield, *Exiles from Paradise,* pp. 91–92

One day in May he was sitting on a bar stool at the Dingo in the rue Delambre, talking to Duff and Pat, when he heard a voice at his elbow. He looked up to see the man [Fitzgerald] who had recommended him to Maxwell Perkins.

Carlos Baker, *Ernest Hemingway: A Life Story,* p. 145

The Dingo Bar, now renamed the Auberge du Centre.

A year later I encountered [Hemingway] in Paris, in a so-called American bar on the Rue Delambre. I was, at the time, engaged in the not uninteresting task of imbibing *fine à l'eau* with Ivan Oppfer. . . . Hemingway joined us and entered the competition.

It appeared that we had numerous mutual friends and enemies, and had seen more or less the same things in the same places. Out of the entire mob then crowded into the café Hemingway looked less like an artist than any of them. He might, from appearance, have been put down as a quarterback from some mid-Western college, the second mate on a coastwise steamer, or the sporting editor of a newspaper. He looked too normal to be a writer.

I attempted to lead him into a conversation regarding his own work, but to no avail. He was more interested in what others were doing, and our conversation ranged from the failing eyesight of James Joyce to the superiority of the white rum found in Guatemala over the calvados of Normandy. A French critic, reviewing some poems of mine that had just been translated, had called me a neo-impressionistic poet, and we both agreed that the critic was a lout and an idiot, and we ordered chili con carne.

Later we went out onto the street to inspect a wheel that Hemingway had just purchased, and on which he intended pedaling to Strasbourg. . . . Our discussion was eventually interrupted by the dramatic appearance of an American girl from the hotel across the way, who announced hysterically that some English boy had just slashed his wrists in an attempt at suicide in her apartment, and for God's sake would somebody do something.

Joseph Hilton Smythe, "Ernest Hemingway
of Boston Put His Playfellows
of Montparnasse into His Stories," p. 3

"I must bathe," said Brett. "Walk up to the hotel with me, Jake. Be a good chap."

"We *have* got the loveliest hotel," Mike said. "I think it's a brothel!"

"We left our bags here at the Dingo when we got in, and they asked us at this hotel if we wanted a room for the afternoon only. Seemed frightfully pleased we were going to stay all night." . . .

We walked up the Rue Delambre.

Hemingway, *The Sun Also Rises,* p. 83

Duff Twysden came only belatedly to a reading of the novel [*The Sun Also Rises*]. Although furious at first, she afterwards relented. When Ernest happened to meet her one night at the Dingo, she said that she had not been at all disturbed. Her only quibble was that she had not in fact slept with the bloody bullfighter.

Carlos Baker, *Ernest Hemingway:
A Life Story,* p. 179

[Hemingway] suggested we go up to the Falstaff, off Montparnasse, an oak-paneled English bar presided over by Jimmy, a friend of his, an Englishman who had been a pro lightweight fighter. At that hour hardly anyone else was in the bar. Behind the bar Jimmy now looked like an amiable roly-poly host. Just a day or two ago I had been asking Jimmy what Lady Duff, the Lady Brett of *The Sun Also Rises,* was really like. Leaning across the bar, Jimmy had said confidentially, "You won't tell Hemingway, will you? No? Well, she was one of those horsey English girls with her hair cut short and the English manner. Hemingway thought she had class. He used to go dancing with her over on the Right Bank. I could never see what he saw in her."

Morley Callaghan,
That Summer in Paris, pp. 126–27

Very soon we were habitués of the Falstaff Bar on the rue du Montparnasse, only a few doors down from the Jules-César. It seemed on the whole better than the Dôme, which was often too noisy, than the Dingo and the Strix, which were too full of alcoholics and Scandinavians respectively, than the College Inn, which though run by Jed Kiley and having a genuine Red Indian barman was too favourite a meeting-place for Americans who really belonged in Harry's New York Bar. Though all these places were amusing and comfortable the Falstaff gained a special charm from the contrast between its rather stuffy oak panelling and padded seats and the haphazard way it was run by the bartender Jimmy Charters, an ex-prizefighter, and the waiter Joe Hildesheim, who came from Brooklyn and was known as Joe the Bum. The Falstaff was owned jointly by two Belgian gentlemen who also shared a mistress, a very plump handsome grey-eyed woman called Madame Mitaine. The three of them sat quietly in the angle of the fireplace every evening and did not interfere in any way, being content to count the cash when the bar closed at two o'clock in the morning. Madame Mitaine would then enter the figures in a little red notebook. Jimmy and Joe ran the place on the principle that about every tenth drink should be on the house, so that regular clients, and still more the casual visitors, were constantly being surprised by a whispered intimation that there was nothing to pay.

John Glassco,
Memoirs of Montparnasse, pp. 29–30

[Ernest, Scott, and I] walked up to the Falstaff. . . . I laughed and said that by tomorrow word would go around the café that I, shamefully, was letting Fitzgerald and Hemingway tell me what to do about a book. Ernest said, "What do you care? We're professionals. We only care whether the thing is as good as it should be."

Morley Callaghan,
That Summer in Paris, p. 219

The Falstaff Bar.

A poster for Le Jockey,
"the best nightclub that ever was."

Walking home at two in the morning we would pass that crowded little dance hall, The Jockey, with the jazz blowing from the open door.

Morley Callaghan,
That Summer in Paris, p. 117

Ernest stopped to study a row of buildings. "In the basement of one of these buildings," he said, "was the best night club that ever was—Le Jockey.

Best orchestra, best drinks, a wonderful clientele, and the world's most beautiful women. Was in there one night with Don Ogden Stewart and Waldo Peirce, when the place was set on fire by the most sensational woman anybody ever saw. Or ever will. Tall, coffee skin, ebony eyes, legs of paradise, a smile to end all smiles. Very hot night but she was wearing a coat of black fur, her breasts handling the fur like it was silk. She turned her eyes on me—she was dancing with the big British gunner subaltern who had brought her—but I responded to the eyes like a hypnotic and cut in on them. The subaltern tried to shoulder me out but the girl slid off him and onto me. Everything under that fur instantly communicated with me. I introduced myself and asked her name. 'Josephine Baker,' she said. We danced nonstop for the rest of the night. She never took off her fur coat. Wasn't until the joint closed she told me she had nothing on underneath."

A. E. Hotchner, *Papa Hemingway,* pp. 52-53

"If you really liked beer, you'd be at Lipp's."
Hemingway, *A Moveable Feast,* p. 102

Lipp's is where you are going to eat and drink too.

It was a quick walk to Lipp's and every place I passed that my stomach noticed as quickly as my eyes or my nose made the walk an added pleasure. There were few people in the *brasserie* and when I sat down on the bench against the wall with the mirror in back and a table in front and the waiter asked if I wanted beer I asked for a *distingué,* the big glass mug that held a liter, and for potato salad.

The beer was very cold and wonderful to drink. The *pommes à l'huile* were firm and marinated and the olive oil delicious. I ground black pepper over the potatoes and moistened the bread in the olive oil. After the first heavy draft of beer I drank and ate very slowly. When the *pommes à l'huile* were gone I ordered another serving and a *cervelas.* This was a sausage like a heavy, wide frankfurter split in two and covered with a special mustard sauce.

I mopped up all the oil and all of the sauce with bread and drank the beer slowly until it began to lose its coldness and then I finished it and ordered a *demi* and watched it drawn. It seemed colder than the *distingué* and I drank half of it.

Hemingway, *A Moveable Feast,* pp. 72–73

. . . then went out to lunch with John Dos Passos . . . We lunched on rollmops, Sole Meunière, Civet de Lièvre à la Chez Cocotte, marmelade de pommes, and washed it all down, as we used to say (eh, reader?) with a bottle of Montrachet 1919, with the sole, and a bottle of Hospice de Beaune 1919 apiece with the jugged hare. Mr. Dos Passos, I believe, shared a bottle of Chambertin with me over the marmelade de pommes (Eng., apple sauce). We drank two vieux marcs, and after deciding not to go to the Café du Dôme and talk about Art we both went to our respective homes and I wrote the following chapter.

Hemingway, *The Torrents of Spring,* p. 68

There's a dim recollection of eating a meal with him and Hadley at Lipp's before there was any Bumby, and of Ernest's talking beautifully about some international conference he'd recently attended. When he was a young man he had one of the shrewdest heads for unmasking political pretensions I've ever run into. . . . I right away put him down as a man with obvious talent for handling the English language.

John Dos Passos, *The Best Times,* p. 141

Harold Loeb, among others [who thought they saw themselves in *The Sun Also Rises*], was said to be out searching for him with a gun. Ernest's response, as he told it, was to send word around the Quarter that he could be found sitting outside Lipp's Brasserie between two and four on certain January afternoons. He took it as a sign of cowardice among his accusers that no bullets whistled.

Carlos Baker, *Ernest Hemingway: A Life Story,* p. 181

Above: A waiter at Brasserie Lipp.
Right: The terrace of the Deux Magots.

St. Germain des Prés with its three cafés, Lipp's, The Flore, and the Deux Magots, is a focal point, the real Paris for illustrious intellectuals. Painters and actors from other capitals, and expensive women came to this neighborhood too. André Gide might be having dinner at the Deux Magots. Picasso had often passed on the street. The Deux Magots, while remaining a neighborhood café, was a center of international Paris life.

Morley Callaghan, *That Summer in Paris,* p. 194

The café des Deux-Magots itself was something like neutral ground, a vague No Man's Land between opposing camps and between the Right Bank and the Left, being a favorite resort of journalists and of Sorbonne professors invading another Bohemia than the one to which they were accustomed in the vicinity of the Boul' Mich'. It was to the Deux-Magots that one took a new acquaintance when uncertain as to just how to place him. The atmosphere as a rule was a tranquil one, a relief to Montparnassians who wanted to get away from it all. Of an afternoon one might find Hemingway there, or Ezra Pound if he happened to be in Paris; and of an evening, Ford Madox Ford would likely be seated at one of the tables, surrounded by a carefully chosen audience of two or three.

Samuel Putnam, *Paris Was Our Mistress*, p. 98

. . . I met Joyce who was walking along the Boulevard St.-Germain after having been to a matinée alone. He liked to listen to the actors, although he could not see them. He asked me to have a drink with him and we went to the Deux-Magots and ordered dry sherry although you will always read that he drank only Swiss white wine.

Hemingway, *A Moveable Feast*, p. 128

In the sunlight on the Deux Magots terrace . . . we found ourselves talking about Ernest. At first it was just an idle conversation. . . . Then [Scott] began to reveal that no matter what might have happened between them, he still kept some wide-eyed loyalty to his own view of Ernest. Whether he was secretly hurt, feeling pushed aside and not needed, didn't matter. He began to tell me about all Ernest's exploits and his prowess and his courage. He told the stories as if he were making simple statements of fact. It seemed to give him pleasure to be able to tell stories about a man whose life was so utterly unlike his own. He gave Ernest's life that touch of glamour that he alone could give, and give better than any man.

Morley Callaghan,
That Summer in Paris, pp. 207–8

Ernest's father had also been a suicide and so had mine, both of the deaths occurring at about the same period of our young lives (I was older than Ernest by seven years), when we were in our twenties. This was a piece of personal duplicate history that he and I had discovered accidentally one day and had discussed with exploratory interest at a quiet back table in the Deux Magots café, which he always favored for serious talk, such as his reading aloud in a rumbling whisper the first poetry he had written after the war.

Janet Flanner, *Paris Was Yesterday,* p. viii

I traveled around Paris with Ernest for a few days. We used to meet in the afternoons at the Café Des Deux Magots, just across the street from our hotel. Pablo Picasso, Janet Flanner, Ginny Cowles, Josephine Herbst, Helen Seldes, Arthur Conan Doyle's son and his White Russian princess wife, and later John Dos Passos and his wife Katie, made up the bulk of our crowd.

Sidney Franklin, *The Bullfighter
from Brooklyn,* pp. 217–18

. . . the old Hole in the Wall bar . . . was a hangout for deserters and for dope peddlers during and after the first war. The Hole in the Wall was a very narrow bar with a red-painted façade, little more than a passageway, on the rue des Italiens. At one time it had a rear exit into the sewers of Paris from which you were supposed to be able to reach the catacombs.

Hemingway, *A Moveable Feast,* p. 143

The entrance to Le Trou dans le Mur is on the Boulevard des Capucines across from the Café de la Paix, but true to its name, you can pass by it a half-dozen times without seeing it. Ernest wanted me to see how he had positioned himself at the back of this mirrored *boîte*—more celebrated in the Twenties than now—whenever vendettas were threatening him. "The day after *The Sun Also Rises* was published," Ernest said, "I got word that Harold Loeb, who was the Robert Cohn of the book, had announced that he would kill me on sight. I sent him a telegram to the effect that I would be here in The Hole in the Wall for three consecutive evenings so he'd have no trouble finding me. As you can see, I chose this joint because it is all mirrors, all four walls, and if you sit in this booth at the back you can see whoever comes in the door and all their moves. I waited out the three days but Harold didn't show. About a week later, I was eating dinner at Lipp's in Saint-Germain, which is also heavily mirrored, when I spotted Harold coming in. I went over and put out my hand and Harold started to shake hands before he remembered we were mortal enemies. He yanked his hand away and put it behind his back. I invited him to have a drink but he refused. 'Never,' is actually what he said. 'Okay,' I said, resuming my seat, 'then drink alone.' He left the restaurant and that was the end of that vendetta."

A. E. Hotchner, *Papa Hemingway,* pp. 47–48

Ernest had been one of Harry's earliest customers [at Harry's New York Bar], and although Ernest did not particularly like the bar any more, because it was "over quaint," he still liked his old friend Harry and went to pay his respects. On the frosted-glass door was the legend: C'EST GENTIL D'ÊTRE VENU. Pennants from American colleges decorated all walls except the one in back of the bar, which was covered with paper money; the face of the cash register was covered with coins; a straw monkey holding boxing gloves dangled from the ceiling above the bar; and a prominent sign exhorted: HELP STAMP OUT SPORTS CARS. "All they need," Ernest said, under his breath, "is Noel Coward leading a community sing." He ordered Scotch and half a fresh lime.

A. E. Hotchner, *Papa Hemingway*, pp. 45–46

Waiters at the Deux Magots.

"Back in the old days this was one of the few good, solid bars, and there was an ex-pug used to come in with a pet lion. He'd stand at the bar here and the lion would stand here beside him. He was a very nice lion with good manners—no growls or roars—but, as lions will, he occasionally shit on the floor. This, of course, had a rather adverse effect on the trade and, as politely as he could, Harry asked the ex-pug not to bring the lion around any more. But the next day the pug was back with the lion, lion dropped another load, drinkers dispersed, Harry again made request. The third day, same thing. Realizing it was do or die for poor Harry's business, this time when the lion let go, I went over, picked up the pug, who had been a welterweight, carried him outside and threw him in the street. Then I came back and grabbed the lion's mane and hustled him out of here. Out on the sidewalk the lion gave me a look, but he went quietly.

"In a crazy way, that's what started me on *A Farewell to Arms*—figured if I was getting that aggressive with lions, time had come to put my juice into a book instead."

A. E. Hotchner, *Papa Hemingway*, p. 46

Zelli's was an extraordinarily successful place and so famous that every American felt obligated to devote at least one of his nights out in Paris to it. Zelli was an American who seemed born to run a night club. He made a particular point of remembering names and developed this talent to so remarkable a degree that he could greet Americans by name from the second visit on. His place was no better than the other tourist traps. In fact it was no different, but it was more fun because of Joe's presence.

The basis of its financial success, as with all other such places, was the sale of ten-franc champagne for two hundred francs. It was served at a temperature just above the freezing point, which made it impossible for even a connoisseur to taste it or to say if it was good or bad. Since the place was full of mirrors and always over-heated and stuffy, people got thirsty and drank plenty of champagne, to say nothing of frequent visits to the bar, where prices were comparable. Zelli's had the exact look of any

night club in New York or London or Shanghai or Berlin.

Like most night clubs in Paris of the 1920's it was full of girls. The girls, who appeared to the casual observer to have dropped in for an evening's dancing, were attached to the place and above the club in most cases, although not at Zelli's, were those rooms so delightfully described as *petits salons particuliers*.

Al Laney, *Paris Herald*, pp. 193–95

Finally we went up to Montmartre. Inside Zelli's it was crowded, smoky, and noisy. The music hit you as you went in. Brett and I danced. It was so crowded we could barely move. The nigger drummer waved at Brett. We were caught in the jam, dancing in one place in front of him.

"Hahre you?"

"Great."

"Thaats good."

He was all teeth and lips.

"He's a great friend of mine," Brett said. "Damn good drummer."

The music stopped and we started toward the table where the count sat. Then the music started again and we danced. I looked at the count. He was sitting at the table smoking a cigar. The music stopped again.

"Let's go over."

Brett started toward the table. The music started and again we danced, tight in the crowd.

"You are a rotten dancer, Jake."

Hemingway, *The Sun Also Rises*, p. 62

. . . famous Prunier, whose sea-food restaurant was the Friday home of all good gourmets in Paris. His Portuguese oysters were one of the modest-priced tasty traditions of France, and his American clientele so numerous that he planted for them local beds of Cape Cod clams and blue points so that Yankees could feel at home at his bar.

Janet Flanner, *Paris Was Yesterday*, pp. 3–4

Above: A restaurant long known for its seafood.
Below: Place de la Concorde from the entrance of Hôtel Crillon.

Another day later that year when we had come back from one of our voyages and had good luck at some track again we stopped at Prunier's on the way home, going in to sit at the bar after looking at all the clearly priced wonders in the window. We had oysters and *crabe Mexicaine* with glasses of Sancerre.

Hemingway, *A Moveable Feast,* p. 53

. . . one day in Paris he saw a man and a woman sitting together upstairs in Prunier's restaurant, and he instantly knew that she had just had an abortion —a scene something like Manet's *L'absinthe,* one imagines. And he thought of himself and his own wife in that situation, not in Prunier's but in a railway station in Spain he happened to know about. Why in Spain? No reason. He called the story *Hills like White Elephants.*

Alan Moorehead, *A Late Education,* p. 159

The three of us went one day around the corner to Prunier's. . . . The elderly waiter pretended to remember Ernest and apologized for the meagerness of the food he could provide us but announced that they still had a good supply of wines. He recommended a Sancerre, the round rich white wine of the Loire, and, whatever its year was, we found it so welcome on our palates that we drank two bottles. . . .

For Ernest's amusement, Marlene [Dietrich] made up ingenue pleasantries. When we were talking about the sea and fishing, she asked, "What is wanting, Papa? Is it pearls, or some kind of fish? I could never understand it."

"Wanting, it's a verb, daughter. An Irish waiter would say, 'What would ye be wanting.' "

"No. No. I meant that thing I've heard—wade and found wanting. That must be in the sea." Laughter and explanation of "weigh."

Mary Welsh Hemingway,
How It Was, pp. 127–28

"When I had money I went to the Crillon."

Hemingway,
A Moveable Feast, p. 192

At five o'clock I was in the Hotel Crillon waiting for Brett. She was not there, so I sat down and wrote some letters. They were not very good letters but I hoped their being on Crillon stationery would help them.

Hemingway, *The Sun Also Rises,* p. 41

"Well, where will I see you?"
"Anywhere around five o'clock."
"Make it the other side of town then."
"Good. I'll be at the Crillon at five."

Hemingway, *The Sun Also Rises,* p. 29

"Where did we stay in Paris?" he asked the woman who was sitting by him in a canvas chair, now, in Africa.
"At the Crillon. You know that."
"Why do I know that?"
"That's where we always stayed."

Hemingway,
"The Snows of Kilimanjaro," p. 57

Scott Fitzgerald invited us to have lunch with his wife Zelda and his little daughter at the furnished flat they had rented at 14 rue Tilsitt. I cannot remember much about the flat except that it was gloomy and airless and that there was nothing in it that seemed to belong to them except Scott's first books bound in light blue leather with the titles in gold.

Hemingway, *A Moveable Feast,* p. 179

. . . the Hemingways went to lunch at the Fitzgeralds' apartment in the rue de Tilsitt. The place struck Ernest as gloomy and sour, and he took an immediate dislike to Zelda, who happened to be suffering from a hangover. She had the eyes of a predatory hawk and spoke jealously of the trip to Lyon as if it had been a huge success. Ernest gathered that she was jealous of the time Scott gave to writing. When he drank she smiled a secret smile which meant, Ernest believed, that she was glad

Scott would not be able to write afterwards. It was not the behavior he cherished in the wife of a writer. But he read *The Great Gatsby* with admiration, and wrote Max Perkins that it was an absolutely first-rate book.

Carlos Baker, *Ernest Hemingway:*
A Life Story, p. 146

The spring of 1925 Gerald Murphy had dropped by Fitzgerald's Paris apartment to find him in a turmoil. "Ernest has just gone home," he said. Apparently Hemingway had been invited to meet Zelda, Fitzgerald assuming they would have everything in common and get along beautifully. The *rapport* had been less than instantaneous—their strong personalities did not blend (Zelda's word for Hemingway was "bogus")—and as Hemingway left, he remarked to Fitzgerald in the hall, "But Scott, you realize, don't you, that she's crazy?"

Andrew Turnbull, *Scott Fitzgerald,* p. 193

Another [note to the reader in *The Torrents of Spring*] mentioned a recent visit from Fitzgerald, who had sat down in the fireplace and refused to let the fire burn anything else but his overcoat. Fitzgerald had in fact appeared sometime after midnight on November 28th. He was so drunk that Ernest had to take him back to his flat in the rue de Tilsitt. On the 30th he sent the Hemingways a note of apology: "It is only fair to say that the deplorable man who entered your apartment Saturday morning was not me but a man named Johnston who has often been mistaken for me."

Carlos Baker,
Ernest Hemingway: A Life Story, p. 159

[Fitzgerald] was always trying to work. Each day he would try and fail. He laid the failure to Paris, the town best organized for a writer to write in that there is . . .

Hemingway, *A Moveable Feast,* p. 182

We had a little party one night in my place—a few American and French friends. During the evening [Hemingway] went to the toilet and came out soon, his head covered with blood. He'd pulled what he thought was the chain, but it was the cord of the casement window above, which came down splintering glass on him. He was bandaged up. I put a small felt hat jauntily on his head partly hiding the bandage—the wound wasn't very serious—and took a picture of him. There have been other pictures of him wounded, before and after this one, but none which gave him the same look of amusement and indifference to the ups and downs of his career. I can imagine the smile on his face, a little more grim perhaps, just before his death recently.

Man Ray, *Self Portrait*, p. 185

Pauline tried to stanch the flow of blood with layers of toilet paper, and then summoned MacLeish, who commandeered a cab. By this time, Ernest was giddy and half-delirious. They reached the American Hospital at Neuilly shortly before three. The intern on duty closed the gaping triangular wound with nine stitches.

Carlos Baker, *Ernest Hemingway: A Life Story*, p. 190

Above: 14, rue Tilsitt, where Fitzgerald had an apartment.
Right: The American Hospital in Neuilly where Hemingway had some stitches taken.

Poor Scott was the despair of a doctor because of his drinking. Hemingway, his fellow novelist, on the other hand, had superb control over himself. I operated on Hemingway for appendicitis. He was a young reporter on the Paris *Herald* at the time, perpetually broke, and he went into the free ward. Only a couple of days after he had been wheeled from the operating room, I was amazed to come across him sitting up in bed with a portable typewriter pounding out a novel *(The Sun Also Rises)*. Not all the king's horses could have separated Hemingway from his typewriter.

Charles F. Bove, *A Paris Surgeon's Story,* p. 60

She found an apartment for herself and Bumby, and F. Puss the cat, at 35, rue de Fleurus, not far from Gertrude Stein.

Alice Sokoloff,
Hadley: The First Mrs. Hemingway, p. 91

While Hadley was away, Ernest stayed with Bumby in the sixth-floor flat. The child spoke French and had many small jokes, such as calling his father Madame Papa. He liked to pretend that a wolf lived in the flat. *"Il n'est pas gentil, le Monsieur Loup-loup,"* said he. When they rode in a cab to some other part of the city, Ernest always asked him, "Where are we now, Schatz?" and Bumby always replied, *"Ici, Papa."* Ernest bought him a harmonica. They sat down at a table in one of the cafés and ordered ice cream. With the ring of vanilla around his mouth, his harmonica clutched in his left hand, and his wide eyes fixed on the passing crowds, Bumby suddenly heaved a great sigh of content-ment. *"Ah,"* said he, *"la vie est beau avec papa."*

Carlos Baker, *Ernest Hemingway:
A Life Story*, pp. 177–78

The finality of his own loss became clear to Ernest when Hadley sent him a list of the items, including furniture, which she wanted him to deliver to her new apartment at 35, rue de Fleurus. He rented a handbarrow and accomplished the move. It required several trips and a separate one for Joan Miró's "The Farm." As he delivered the first of his loads he burst into tears.

Carlos Baker, *Ernest Hemingway:
A Life Story*, p. 177

Hadley moved to this building at 35 rue de Fleurus, when she and Hemingway parted, but the part where she lived has been removed.

Don [Stewart] was dismayed at the ruin of a mar-riage which he had thought indestructible. So were the Murphys. On learning that Hadley and Ernest were going to set up separate residences, Gerald offered Ernest the use of a studio he was leasing at 69, rue Froidevaux. . . . Ernest settled into Gerald's studio and began to read proof on *The Sun Also Rises.*

Carlos Baker, *Ernest Hemingway:
A Life Story*, pp. 172–73

He really worked hard. I went around to the ceme-tery room one day to see him. The concierge told me he was there. So I climbed the five flights and rapped on his door but he wouldn't let me in. The under-taker's assistant who had the room next to him told

on the house next door that flashed on and off. It said *Pompes Funèbres.* Clever idea for an undertaker, I thought. . . . The house on the other side had a marble orchard in the front yard. It was a monument maker's atelier. The stone angels and other tombstones jumped at you when the undertaker's sign lit up. Nice cheerful spot, I thought. He hopped out like he was going in to the Louvre Palace.

"My room's on the fifth floor, girls," he said. "Come up and see me some time."

"Rest in peace," I said.

Jed Kiley, *Hemingway: An Old Friend Remembers,* pp. 45–46

After separating from Hadley, Hemingway worked in a studio here at 69, rue Froideveaux, in a part of the building that no longer stands.

me he had been locked in his room for a week correcting proofs. Wouldn't let anybody in. They used to leave coffee and croissants at the door for him. The only exercise he got was walking to the bathroom at the other end of the hall. If genius is really the capacity for taking infinite pains, he *is* a genius, I thought.

Jed Kiley, *Hemingway: An Old Friend Remembers,* p. 47

"Turn left at the cemetery," . . .

"Third house from the corner," he said.

I stopped at the third house. It was an old brick relic of the Second Empire. It had a *Chambres à louer* sign in the window and was right across the street from the cemetery. . . . There was a big electric sign

I happened to be with him on the day he turned down an offer from one of Mr. Hearst's editors, which, had he accepted it, would have supported him handsomely for years. He was at the time living back of the Montparnasse cemetery over the studio of a friend, in a room small and bare except for a bed and table, and buying his midday meal for five sous from street vendors of fried potatoes.

John Peale Bishop,
"Homage to Hemingway," p. 39

He lived at 6 rue Férou, which was within a quarter of a mile of the St. Sulpice Cathedral. . . . He had a living room off a narrow room with a long oaken table, and, I suppose, a kitchen and some bedrooms. On the wall was a Joan Miró painting of a fish. The great Miró was his friend, he said. With some pride he showed us a small Goya he had been able to smuggle out of Spain.

Morley Callaghan,
That Summer in Paris, p. 97

After you came out of the Luxembourg you could walk down the narrow rue Férou to the Place St.-Sulpice and there were still no restaurants, only the quiet square with its benches and trees. There was a fountain with lions, and pigeons walked on the pavement and perched on the statues of the bishops. There was the church and there were shops selling religious objects and vestments on the north side of the square.

Hemingway, *A Moveable Feast,* pp. 69–70

A view down rue Férou toward St.-Sulpice.

Above: Place St.-Sulpice. *Right:* Religious figures in a shop window near St.-Sulpice.

SPORTS

It is easy to say that he is very tall, and as proportionately broad, and that he has brown eyes and always looks serious unless he is boxing, or ski-ing or playing tennis or swimming or boxing or drinking or eating or talking. That is not enough. There is a terrific vitality . . .

Philip Jordan, "Ernest Hemingway:
A Personal Study," p. 541

We went downstairs and into a back room that had a cement floor. In one corner of the room were some mats and the parallel bars. This was the room the members evidently used for a little gym exercise. . . . Ernest and I stripped down to our shorts and shirts. I tied on my espadrilles, he put on his gym shoes. We began to box.

Morley Callaghan,
That Summer in Paris, pp. 103–4

Now Hemingway in his turn loved boxing. Every chance he got he must have boxed with someone, and he had all the lingo, he had hung around gyms, he had watched fighters at work. Something within him drove him to want to be expert at every occupation he touched. In those days he liked telling a man how to do things, but not by way of boasting or arrogance—it was almost as if he had to feel he had a sense of professionalism about every field of human behavior that interested him.

Morley Callaghan,
That Summer in Paris, p. 124

There was a gymnasium in the rue Pontoise where he often went to earn ten francs a round by sparring with professional heavyweights. The job called for a nice blend of skill and forbearance, since hirelings must be polite while fighting back just enough to engage, without enraging, the emotions of the fighters.

Carlos Baker, *Ernest Hemingway:
A Life Story,* p. 126

Due, no doubt, to Miró's presence, it was one of our best boxing afternoons. At other times in our boxing Ernest and I would laugh and kid each other. Miró added a touch of solemn Spanish dignity to the affair. Taking off his neat coat, he carefully folded it. Moving with brusque efficiency, he studied his watch so he could call out accurately the beginning of the three-minute round and the minute rest. All his movements became precise, stern, polite and yet dominating. Never had I had a timekeeper so immersed in a match, and so commanding with his splendid dignified earnestness. To have laughed or not been workmanlike in our boxing would have been an insult to his dignity; he would have been disappointed in us. So it was a good afternoon. We were all happy and satisfied, and I thought that Miró, especially, had enjoyed himself.

Morley Callaghan,
That Summer in Paris, p. 168

Scott sat down on the bench by the wall, while Ernest and I stripped. Then Ernest had him take out his watch and gave him his instructions. A round was to be three minutes, then a minute for a rest. . . .

Right at the beginning of that [second] round Ernest got careless; he came in too fast, his left down, and he got smacked on the mouth. His lip began to bleed. It had often happened. It should have meant nothing to him. . . . Out of the corner of his eye he may have seen the shocked expression on Scott's face. Or the taste of blood in his mouth may have made him want to fight more savagely. He came lunging in, swinging more recklessly. As I circled around him, I kept jabbing at his bleeding mouth. I had to forget all about Scott, for Ernest had become rougher, his punching a little wilder than usual. His heavy punches, if they had landed, would have stunned me. I had to punch faster and harder myself to keep away from him. It bothered me that he was taking the punches on the face like a man telling himself he only needed to land one big punch himself.

. . . I was wondering why I was tiring, for I hadn't been hit solidly. Then Ernest, wiping the blood from his mouth with his glove, and probably made careless with exasperation and embarrassment from having Scott there, came leaping in at me.

Stepping in, I beat him to the punch. The timing must have been just right. I caught him on the jaw; spinning around he went down, sprawled out on his back.

. . . "Oh, my God!" Scott cried suddenly. When I looked at him, alarmed, he was shaking his head helplessly. "I let the round go four minutes," he said.

A Parisian gym.

"Christ!" Ernest yelled. He got up. He was silent for a few seconds. Scott, staring at his watch, was mute and wondering. I wished I were miles away. "All right, Scott," Ernest said savagely, "if you want to see me getting the shit knocked out of me, just say so. Only don't say you made a mistake," and he stomped off to the shower room to wipe the blood from his mouth.

Morley Callaghan,
That Summer in Paris, pp. 212–14

Some months later when Fitzgerald, in a drunken quarrel, said he felt a need to smash Hemingway as a man, Hemingway suggested that Fitzgerald had

purposely let the round go on. Fitzgerald was so indignant that Hemingway wrote a long letter exonerating him. Meanwhile the *New York Herald Tribune* had printed a false report that Callaghan had knocked Hemingway out. Hemingway prevailed on Fitzgerald to wire Callaghan (now in America) that he, Fitzgerald, was awaiting a correction of the story. Callaghan, who hadn't been responsible for the story in the first place and who had already sent in a correction, was incensed at Fitzgerald until Hemingway wrote him, taking full responsibility for the wire.

Andrew Turnbull, *Scott Fitzgerald,* pp. 190–91

On September 24, 1922, before leaving Paris for Constantinople to cover the Greco-Turkish War, Hemingway attended a murderous fight between Battling Siki and Georges Carpentier for the lightheavyweight championship of the world. . . .

Battling Siki was a Senegalese lightheavyweight of some small renown, and in 1922 Hemingway wrote to his brother that he and Ezra Pound had seen Siki, who Hemingway believed would become world champion if he would stop training in cafés. Siki, indeed, trained on absinthe. He must have made quite an impression on Hemingway, as he did on everyone else, as Siki regularly made the rounds of the Paris bistros with a lion in tow. (After the Carpentier fight Siki added a monkey, which perched on his shoulder.)

This was the fighter that Hemingway saw enter the ring at the new Mont Rouge arena in Paris, to meet Georges Carpentier, the lightheavyweight champion of the world. . . . Suffice it to say that Siki was supposed to lose the fight, and decided in the ring to pull a double-cross. He fairly battered Carpentier into oblivion. Then, at the moment of the crucial knockdown, the referee stepped in suddenly and stopped the fight, awarding it to Carpentier on a foul. The referee's act started the hundreds of Americans at ringside to shouting "robber." . . . The crowd at the arena became so threatening that the fight officials rescinded the decision of the referee and awarded the bout to Siki. Later Siki himself related how the bout was framed. The Siki-Carpentier battle, which was designed to be the "frame-up of the century," became the greatest double-cross in fight history, and it is difficult to think that so famous a fight, with a double-cross, that Hemingway attended, played no part in the plot of "Fifty Grand."

James J. Martine,
"Hemingway's 'Fifty Grand':
The Other Fight(s)," pp. 124–25

One evening our educators, Hemingway and Hadley, stopped by for us and we all set off by Métro to the mountainous region of Ménilmontant, inhabited by workers, sportsmen, and a certain number of toughs. . . .

[The] last fight led to another—in which the spectators participated. . . . What with the socking, the kicking, the yelling, and the surging back and forth, I was afraid we would be "Hemmed" in, and that Hadley would be injured in the melee. Calls for *"le flic! le flic!"* were heard, but evidently not by the cop whose attendance at all French places of amusement, whether it's the Comédie Francaise or a box-

ing ring in Ménilmontant, is obligatory. We heard Hemingway's voice above the din exclaiming with disapproval: *"Et naturellement le flic est dans la pissottière!"*

Sylvia Beach,
Shakespeare and Company, pp. 79–80

We became friendly; one night he took me to an important boxing match; I wasn't interested in sports myself, but seized the occasion to try out a new hand movie camera I had acquired. . . . Ernest and I were in the fourth or fifth row, while my assistant was in front near the ring, for closeups. When the first round started, the latter raised his camera and had hardly run off a few feet when the manager rushed over and yanked it out of his hands. I discreetly raised my camera and started it rolling. Before I had run off the thirty feet of film there was a dramatic knockout—in the first round. Pandemonium broke out in the hall, Hemingway joining in the shouting and the arm-waving. The next day I went to the manager's office to claim my assistant's camera. The manager returned it, first confiscating the film. No pictures were allowed, he said. I returned to my studio, developed the film in my own camera and furnished the illustrated weekly with pictures of a sensational knockout. . . . Hemingway loved boxing; when he had no one else to spar with, he took on Joan Miró, the Spanish painter, more than a head shorter than himself. When he had no one at all, he'd put a pair of baby boxing gloves on his little boy Bumby's hands, and box with him holding him in his arms.

Man Ray, *Self Portrait,* pp. 184–85

. . . the great twenty-round fights at the Cirque d'Hiver.

Hemingway, *A Moveable Feast,* preface

He was also a frequent visitor to the prizefights in the Cirque de Paris, keeping an eye on a colored fighter named Larry Gains, in whom he had taken an interest, and using press tickets supplied by Bird and Hickok.

Carlos Baker, *Ernest Hemingway:
A Life Story,* p. 127

The Hemingways attended boxing matches at the Cirque d'Hiver.

He asked me not to miss the boxing matches at the Cirque d'Hiver, and Hadley described the match they had seen the night before, using boxing terms as technical as her husband's.

Burton Rascoe, *We Were Interrupted,* p. 186

Take the time at the Vélodrome d'Hiver. It happened at one of their weekly fights. . . . Who do you suppose was the only one to take my part? Right. Monsieur Hemingway. He appeared from nowhere. He was grinning from ear to ear. But he wasn't fooling. He grabbed the two pugs, each by an arm, and pulled the two of them from me as though they were babies. "Get the sponge," he said. "I'll take care of these two punks." . . . When I returned to raise Hemingway's hand he was gone. He had disappeared as mysteriously as he had appeared.

What a strange mixture of guts and diffidence, I thought. He had not hesitated to take a hand in a friend's quarrel in front of the whole crowd. Might even have caused a riot if someone had started swinging. Then the minute the danger is over he fades out of the picture. Funny guy, all right.

Jed Kiley, *Hemingway:
An Old Friend Remembers,* pp. 37–39

Then they were off in a jump and out of sight behind the trees and the gong going for dear life and the pari-mutuel wickets rattling down. Gosh, I was so excited, I was afraid to look at them, but I fixed the glasses on the place where they would come out back of the trees and then out they came with the old black jacket going third and they all sailing over the jump like birds. Then they went out of sight again and then they came pounding out and down the hill and all going nice and sweet and easy and taking the fence smooth in a bunch, and moving away from us all solid. Looked as though you could walk across on their backs they were all so bunched and going so smooth. Then they bellied over the big double Bullfinch and something came down. I couldn't see who it was, but in a minute the horse was up and galloping free and the field, all bunched still, sweeping around the long left turn into the straightaway. They jumped the stone wall and came jammed down the stretch toward the big water-jump right in front of the stands. I saw them coming and hollered at my old man as he went by, and he was leading by about a length and riding way out, and light as a monkey, and they were racing for the water-jump. They took off over the big hedge of the water-jump in a pack and then there was a crash, and two horses pulled sideways out off it, and kept on going, and three

others were piled up. I couldn't see my old man anywhere.

Hemingway, "My Old Man," pp. 203–4

It was a hazy day the way it is in the fall when it's blue smoky looking and we were in the upper stand right opposite the water jump and on our left was the bullfinch and the stone wall. The finish was on the side closer to us and the water jump was on the inner course of the track.

Hemingway, *Islands in the Stream,* p. 187

"Do you remember when we'd be down on the rail, Audrey, and how after the horses came over the last obstacle they would be coming straight down toward us and the way they would look coming bigger and bigger and the noise they would make on the turf when they would go past?"

Hemingway, *Islands in the Stream,* p. 188

We went racing together many more times that year and other years after I had worked in the early mornings, and Hadley enjoyed it and sometimes she loved it. . . .

Racing never came between us, only people

A steeplechase at Auteuil.

could do that; but for a long time it stayed close to us like a demanding friend. That was a generous way to think of it. I, the one who was so righteous about people and their destructiveness, tolerated this friend that was the falsest, most beautiful, most exciting, vicious, and demanding because she could be profitable. To make it profitable was more than a full-time job and I had no time for that. But I justified it to myself because I wrote it. . . .

I worked two tracks in their season when I could, Auteuil and Enghien. . . .

You had to watch a jumping race from the top of the stands at Auteuil and it was a fast climb up to see what each horse did and see the horse that might have won and did not, and see why or maybe how he did not do what he could have done. You watched the prices and all the shifts of odds each time a horse you were following would start, and you had to know how he was working and finally get to know when the stable would try with him. He always might be beaten when he tried; but you should know by then what his chances were. It was hard work but at Auteuil it was beautiful to watch each day they raced when you could be there and see the honest races with the great horses, and you got to know the course as well as any place you had ever known. You knew many people finally, jockeys and trainers and owners and too many horses and too many things.

In principle I only bet when I had a horse to bet on but I sometimes found horses that nobody believed in except the men who trained and rode them that won race after race with me betting on them. I stopped finally because it took too much time . . .

Hemingway, *A Moveable Feast,* pp. 61–62

"But wasn't Auteuil a beautiful track though?"
Hemingway, *Islands in the Stream,* p. 187

"You couldn't expect me to look like a colt forever. Do you remember when you told me I looked like a colt at Auteuil that time and I cried?"
Hemingway, *Islands in the Stream,* p. 184

Overleaf: The stands at Auteuil, before World War I.

One day at Auteuil, after a selling steeplechase, my old man bought in the winner for 30,000 francs. He had to bid a little to get him but the stable let the horse go finally and my old man had his permit and his colors in a week. Gee, I felt proud when my old man was an owner.

Hemingway, "My Old Man," p. 202

I do not expect ever to duplicate the pleasure of those Paris steeplechase days. The Degas horses and jockeys against a Renoir landscape; Ernest's silver flask, engraved "From Mary with Love" and containing splendidly aged Calvados; the boisterous excitement of booting home a winner, the glasses zeroed on the moving point, the insistent admonitions to the jockey; the quiet intimacy of Ernest's nostalgia. "You know, Hotch, one of the things I liked best in life was to wake early in the morning with the birds singing and the windows open and the sound of horses jumping." We were sitting on the top steps of the grandstand, the weather damp, Ernest wrapped in his big trench coat, a knitted tan skullcap on his head, his beard close-cropped. . . . We were not betting on the seventh race and Ernest was leaning forward, a pair of rented binoculars swinging from his neck, watching the horses slowly serpentine onto the track from the paddock. "When I was young here," he said, "I was the only outsider who was allowed into the private training grounds at Achères, outside of Maisons-Laffitte, and Chantilly. They let me clock the workouts—almost no one but owners were allowed to operate a stopwatch—and it gave me a big jump on my bets. That's how I came to know about Epinard. A trainer named J. Patrick, an expatriate American who had been a friend of mine since the time we were both kids in the Italian army, told me that Gene Leigh had a colt that might be the horse of the century. Those were Patrick's words, 'the horse of the century.' He said, 'Ernie, he's the son of Badajoz-Epine Blanche, by Rockminster, and nothing like him has been seen in France since the days of Gladiateur and La Grande Ecurie. So take my advice—beg, borrow or steal all the cash you can get your hands on and get it down on this two-year-old for the first start. After that there'll never be odds

again. But that first start, before they know that name, get down on him.'

"It was my 'complete poverty' period—I didn't even have milk money for Bumby, but I followed Patrick's advice. I hit everyone for cash. I even borrowed a thousand francs from my barber. I accosted strangers. There wasn't a sou in Paris that hadn't been nailed down that I didn't solicit; so I was really 'on' Epinard when he started in the Prix Yacoulef at Deauville for his debut. His price was fifty-nine to ten. He won in a breeze, and I was able to support myself for six or eight months on the winnings.

Contemporary views of Auteuil from the restaurant and from the stands.

Patrick introduced me to many insiders of the top French race-set of that time. Frank O'Neill, Frank Keogh, Jim Winkfield, Sam Bush and the truly great steeplechase rider Georges Parfremont."

"How can you remember their names after all these years?" I asked. "Have you seen them since?"

"No. I have always made things stick that I wanted to stick. I've never kept notes or a journal. I just push the recall button and there it is. If it isn't there, it wasn't worth keeping."

A. E. Hotchner, *Papa Hemingway,* pp. 37–39

"There's a beauty restaurant at the top, hung right over the track, where you can eat good and watch them as though you were riding in the race. They bring you the *cote jaune* with the changing odds three times for each race, and you can bet right there, no rushing up and down to the bet cages with your unsettled food jiggling. It's too easy, but wonderful for scouting a race."

A. E. Hotchner, *Papa Hemingway,* p. 36

After Rickey left we went into the bar, where Ernest ordered Scotch with a half a lime squeezed into it and I ordered a split of champagne. "Hell of a boy, that Rickey," he said. "He did some things . . ." His thoughts took him away and he sipped his Scotch, holding each sip in his mouth to warm it and taste it before swallowing. He took from his pocket the pencil stub that he had been using to mark his racing form, and he began to write on the back of a paper napkin. The last race ended and the bar filled and got noisy, but Ernest wrote in deep concentration, oblivious to the post-race commotion. He ordered another Scotch and continued to write, balling up one napkin after another and tossing them under the table. There were only a few of us left in the bar when he finally put the pencil back into his pocket. He handed me the napkin. He had written a sixteen-line poem, "Across the Board," which interwove his remembrance of Rickey with the sounds of the track.

A. E. Hotchner, *Papa Hemingway*, pp. 41–42

The last week of the Auteuil meet we audited the Hemhotch books and found we were running slightly ahead, but considering the time, skill, emotion and energy which had gone into our Steeplechase Devotional, "slightly" was hardly proper compensation. Two days before the end of the meet, however, on December 21st to be exact, as it sometimes happens to horse players, our fortunes dramatically surged upward.

It began with a phone call at six in the morning.

"This is Hemingstein the Tout. Are you awake?"

"No."

"Then get awake. This is a big day. I have just had word from Georges that there is a good horse in today's race, the first one that Georges really believes in, and I think we better meet earlier than usual and give it our special attention." Ernest was referring to Georges, the Ritz's *chef du bar*, who was a very cautious track scholar, so this development had to be treated seriously. . . .

Ernest told me the name of the horse was Bataclan II, that the word was that he had previously performed under wraps but was now going to be given its head for the first time; the odds were twenty-seven to one. He had already gathered and studied every available piece of information about Bataclan's past performances, had checked him out favorably with his jockey-room contacts, and had come to the conclusion that we should shoot the entire contents of our treasury and whatever other capital we could raise on the nose of this jumper. . . .

Ernest was deep in consultation with Georges when I arrived. Bloody Marys to one side, the table top was a morass of charts, forms, scribbles and whatnot. The "thorough briefing" was one of Ernest's most salient characteristics, and it applied to everything he did. His curiosity and sense of pursuit would send him swimming through schools of minutiae which would flow into his maw and emerge crystalized on the pages of *Death in the Afternoon* or "Big Two-Hearted River" or in his flawless techniques for deep-sea fishing and big-game hunting. Now he was in pursuit of Bataclan II.

Apologetically I placed my rather meager collection of franc notes on the table. Ernest pulled a sheet of paper out from under the others and added my amount to a list. "We have more contributors," he said, "than a numbers drop in the Theresa Hotel on a Saturday afternoon. Every waiter in the joint has something down, plus Georges, plus Bertin, Miss Mary, Jigee, the concierge at the Rue Cambon entrance, Claude the groom, and Maurice the men's-room attendant. If Bataclan doesn't perform as expected, we better check into another hotel tonight." . . .

But again he was interrupted, this time by the arrival of a short plump man in clerical robes who called out, "Don Ernesto!"

"Black Priest!" Ernest exclaimed, and he arose and embraced him Spanish-fashion. Black Priest, on a month's sabbatical, had arrived in Paris on his way to a little town in the north of France where he was about to invest his modest life's savings in a new ceramic factory that was being started by a Frenchman he had met in Cuba. He had some reservations about the trustworthiness of his new partner, as did Ernest, but Black Priest felt it was worth the risk since it was his only chance of emancipation. He sat at the table and drank a Bloody Mary and watched in wonderment as Ernest wound up our pretrack conference with a final audit of the funds to be bet. "I'm sorry to have to run off, Black Priest," Ernest said, "but we have this titanic track venture under way. Please have dinner with us tonight at eight o'clock."

"Don Ernesto," Black Priest said solemnly in Spanish, "I have been listening to the nature of your operation, and I would like to come to the track with you and invest my ceramic money in your race horse instead."

"I'm sorry," Ernest answered in Spanish, "but I could not accept the responsibility for such risk."

A rather heated discussion followed, Black Priest insisting, Ernest refusing, until a compromise was reached that Black Priest was to bet only half his ceramic money on Bataclan II. . . .

Ernest went down to the paddock and studied our horse and the other horses as they paraded by; later, when we were in the grandstand and Bataclan came onto the track he said, "The ones we have to worry about are Klipper and Killibi. That Killibi has a good smell. But, as you know, the thing that really spooks me is that goddamn last jump."

The cockney-speaking tout and his pal, whom we had previously encountered, now approached Ernest and offered him a guaranteed, certified mount, but he demurred. I waited until the last moment to get our bets down; we were betting so heavily I didn't want the tote board to show it before closing. The final odds were nineteen to one. I got back to the stands just as the horses broke away. Bataclan ran first, then faded to second on the upgraded backstretch; he lost more ground on the water jump, and on the turn it was Killibi, Klipper and Bataclan in that order. As they came toward us going into the last jump, Bataclan was a hopeless twenty lengths off the pace. I moaned. "Keep your glasses on them," Ernest commanded.

As Killibi took the low hedge, pressed by Klipper, his jockey reached for the bat and in so doing loosened his grip. Killibi's front legs dropped slightly and scraped the hedge, breaking his stride, and he hit the turf hard and stumbled and pitched forward with his boy jumping clear. Klipper was already through the jump at the fall; his jockey tried to clear the fallen Killibi but he couldn't make it and Klipper went right down on top of Killibi, the jock hitting the turf hard and not moving.

Bataclan's jockey had plenty of time to see what had happened and he took Bataclan to the opposite side of the hedge for his jump and came in five lengths to the good.

Nobody in our party made any effort to subdue his feelings. We started a jubilant exodus to the bar, but along the way Black Priest suddenly stopped and refused to budge. He just stood there, looking determined. "Not yet," he kept saying. "Not yet." When the stands around us had emptied, he gave a quick look around and then moved his foot off a Bataclan win ticket it had been covering. "No doubt about it," Ernest said, "God is everywhere."

I took all tickets to the cashier while the others went off to the bar for champagne, and what I returned with was a Matterhorn of ten-thousand-franc notes. Ernest peeled off Black Priest's winnings and gave them to him. "Black Priest needs the bird in hand," he said. "He's been in the bush too long." As always Ernest was wearing his special race-track jacket, a heavy tweed coat that had been made for him when he was in Hong Kong, and which contained a very deep inside pocket that had an elaborate series of buttons which reputedly made it pickpocket proof, even by Hong Kong standards. Into it he stuffed all our loot and it made him look like a side-pregnant bear. As Ernest was stacking the money, the two touts who had approached us earlier went by. "Ah," one of them said to Ernest, tipping his hat, "one can see that Monsieur is of the *métier*."

A. E. Hotchner, *Papa Hemingway*, pp. 58–63

I remember a horse named Bataclan. He was racing in Paris in about '53 or '54. He gave us a marvelous win, though that day I didn't go. . . . When they got back I noticed that Ernest and Hotch looked sort of stuffed—you know, twice their normal size, in their trench coats. And then they began to pull bundles of those huge one-thousand and five-thousand and ten-thousand franc notes from their pockets and throw them on the pink silk coverlet on the bed. . . . This was at the Ritz, in Paris. Well, it made a six-foot yard-high hill of loot! I'd never seen so much cash in my life. And then Ernest picked up a cane. My friend Gigi Viertel was with me. And Ernest slashed into the pile of banknotes. He swished about a fourth of them onto the floor and said, "One for Gigi." Then he pushed another quarter onto the floor and said, "And this one is for Miss Mary." The third quarter was for Hotch and the fourth for Ernest.

Mary Welsh Hemingway,
"A Redbook Dialogue," p. 63

I decided to go down and buy a morning racing paper. There was no quarter too poor to have at least one copy of a racing paper but you had to buy it early on a day like this. I found one in the rue Descartes at the corner of the Place Contrescarpe. . . . [Before] I started work again I looked at the paper. They were running at Enghien, the small, pretty and larcenous track that was the home of the outsider.

So that day after I had finished work we would go racing. Some money had come from the Toronto paper that I did newspaper work for and we wanted a long shot if we could find one. My wife had a horse one time at Auteuil named Chèvre d'Or that was a hundred and twenty to one and leading by twenty lengths when he fell at the last jump with enough savings on him to keep us six months. We tried never to think of that. We were ahead on that year until Chèvre d'Or.

"Do we have enough money to really bet, Tatie?" my wife asked.

"No. We'll just figure to spend what we take. Is there something else you'd rather spend it for?"

"Well," she said. . . .

The racecourse at Enghien-Les-Bains.

So we went out by train from the Gare du Nord through the dirtiest and saddest part of town and walked from the siding to the oasis of the track. It was early and we sat on my raincoat on the fresh cropped grass bank and had our lunch and drank from the wine bottle and looked at the old grandstand, the brown wooden betting booths, the green of the track, the darker green of the hurdles, and the brown shine of the water jumps and the whitewashed stone walls and white posts and rails, the paddock under the new leafed trees and the first horses being walked to the paddock. We drank more wine and studied the form in the paper and my wife lay down on the raincoat to sleep with the sun on her face. I went over and found someone I knew from the old days at San Siro in Milano. He gave me two horses.

"Mind, they're no investment. But don't let the price put you off."

We won the first with half of the money that we had to spend and he paid twelve to one, jumping beautifully, taking command on the far side of the course and coming in four lengths ahead. We saved half of the money and put it away and bet the other half on the second horse who broke ahead, led all the way over the hurdles and on the flat just lasted to the finish line with the favorite gaining on him with every jump and the two whips flailing.

We went to have a glass of champagne at the bar under the stand and wait for the prices to go up.

"My, but racing is very hard on people," my wife said. "Did you see that horse come up on him?"

"I can still feel it inside me."

"What will he pay?"

"The *cote* was eighteen to one. But they may have bet him at the last."

The horses came by, ours wet, with his nostrils working wide to breathe, the jockey patting him.

"Poor him," my wife said. "We just bet."

We watched them go on by and had another glass of champagne and then the winning price came up: 85. That meant he paid eighty-five francs for ten.

"They must have put a lot of money on at the end," I said.

But we had made plenty of money, big money for us, and now we had spring and money too. I thought that was all we needed.

Hemingway, *A Moveable Feast*, pp. 49–53

A newsstand that sells racing sheets.

I have started many stories about bicycle racing but have never written one that is as good as the races are both on the indoor and outdoor tracks and on the roads. But I will get the Vélodrome d'Hiver with the smoky light of the afternoon and the high-banked wooden track and the whirring sound the tires made on the wood as the riders passed, the effort and the tactics as the riders climbed and plunged, each one a part of his machine; I will get the magic of the *demi-fond,* the noise of the motors with their rollers set out behind them that the *entraîneurs* rode, wearing their heavy crash helmets and leaning backward in their ponderous leather suits, to shelter the riders who followed them from the air resistance, the riders in their lighter crash helmets bent low over their handlebars their legs turning the huge gear sprockets and the small front wheels touching the roller behind the machine that gave them shelter to ride in, and the duels that were more exciting than anything, the *put-put*ing of the motorcycles and the riders elbow to elbow and wheel to wheel up and down and around at deadly speed until one man could not hold the pace and broke away and the solid wall of air that he had been sheltered against hit him.

Hemingway, *A Moveable Feast,* pp. 64–65

There were so many kinds of racing. The straight sprints raced in heats or in match races where the two riders would balance for long seconds on their machines for the advantage of making the other rider take the lead and then the slow circling and the final plunge into the driving purity of speed. There were the programs of the team races of two hours, with a series of pure sprints in their heats to fill the afternoon, the lonely absolute speed events of one man racing an hour against the clock, the terribly dangerous and beautiful races of one hundred kilometers on the big banked wooden five-hundred-meter bowl of the Stade Buffalo, the outdoor stadium at Montrouge where they raced behind big motorcycles, . . . and the championships of France behind big motors of the six-hundred-and-sixty-meter cement track of the Parc du Prince near Auteuil, the wickedest track of all . . .

Hemingway, *A Moveable Feast,* p. 65

Ernest found a new sporting interest that year, the six-day bicycle races. They would leave the baby with Marie Cocotte and arrive at the Vélodrome d'Hiver armed with cushions, sandwiches and a thermos of coffee, staying sometimes through the whole night, with Hadley curled up on the bench for naps.

Alice Sokoloff,
Hadley: The First Mrs. Hemingway, p. 73

I did enjoy going to the sixday bicycle races with him. The Six Jours at the Vélo d'Hiver was fun. French sporting events had for me a special comical air that I enjoyed. We would collect, at the stalls and barrows of one of the narrow market streets we both loved, a quantity of wine and cheeses and crunchy rolls, a pot of paté and perhaps a cold chicken, and sit up in the gallery. Hem knew all the statistics and the names and lives of the riders. His enthusiasm was catching but he tended to make a business of it while I just liked to eat and drink and to enjoy the show.

John Dos Passos, *The Best Times,* p. 143

His Sundays that fall [1929] combined duty and pleasure—Mass at St. Sulpice with Pauline, followed by the six-day bicycle races at the Vélodrome d'Hiver.

Carlos Baker, *Ernest Hemingway:
A Life Story,* p. 205

A six-day bicycle race in a stadium, around 1930.

THE LIBERATION
AND THE

OF PARIS
LATER YEARS

"As we [Hemingway, Bruce, Pelkey, and others] went down the hill toward the Seine . . . the streets were lined with people. All houses were gay with flags, and the population almost hysterical with joy. Our progress was extremely slow, and there were many long halts as road blocks were cleared, or small points of enemy resistance eliminated. During these stops we were mobbed by the bystanders. . . . When they knew we were Americans, that seemed to increase their enthusiasm."

Colonel David Bruce quoted in Carlos Baker,
Ernest Hemingway: A Life Story, p. 415

"[Hemingway and Bruce] walked across . . . to the Tomb of the Unknown Soldier. It was being guarded by six veterans, standing at attention, and a mutilated ex-soldier, seated in a wheelchair. . . . The French Captain in charge asked us if we wanted to ascend to the roof of the Arc. We did so and were greeted by a squad of Pompiers standing at attention. For some reason, their Commander presented me with a pompier's medal. . . . At the end of the Champs Élysées a vehicle was burning in the Place de la Concorde and behind, in the Tuileries Gardens, it looked as if a tank was on fire. Smoke was issuing from the Crillon Hotel and, across the river, from the Chamber of Deputies. Snipers were firing steadily into the area around the Arc de Triomphe, and French were firing back at them. . . . The view [from the top] was breathtaking. One saw the golden dome of the Invalides, the green roof of the Madeleine, Sacré-Coeur, and other familiar landmarks. Tanks were firing in various streets. Part of the Arc was under fire from snipers. A shell from a German 88 nicked one of its sides."

Colonel David Bruce quoted in Carlos Baker,
Ernest Hemingway: A Life Story, p. 416

The Arc de Triomphe during the Allied liberation.

158

There, fittingly enough, Hemingway assisted in the liberation of the Travellers' Club, considered doing the same for the Guaranty Trust Company of New York at 4, place de la Concorde, from which they were deterred both by its sturdy doors and by the concentration of German fire from the Ministry of Marine just across the rue Royale, and then went by way of the place de la Concorde through the Tuileries to the place Vendôme where, as Hemingway jocularly said, they "liberated" the Ritz Hotel.

Carlos Baker, *Hemingway and His Critics*, p. 7

Above: The Travellers' Club. *Right:* Awnings of the Ritz Hotel.

On many later occasions, Ernest asserted that he had personally liberated the Travellers Club. What actually happened, after an interlude of champagne drinking, was that Hemingway, Bruce, and Pelkey, finding the Champs Élysées completely bare of traffic, drove at breakneck speed down the broad avenue and pulled up at the Club door. All the rooms were closed except the bar, where the Club president, an elderly Frenchman, was stationed with a number of the Old Guard. Since the Americans were the first outsiders to reach the Club, a testimonial bottle of champagne was quickly opened and toasts offered. As they drank, a sniper began to fire from an adjoining roof.

Carlos Baker, *Ernest Hemingway:
A Life Story,* p. 416

A few blocks away, two truckloads of FFI drove up at the main entrance of an equally famous Paris hostelry. Dirty and dusty, in berets, undershirts, and grease-stained blue-denim work clothes, they strode like the workers' battalions that had marched out to defend Madrid into the very citadel of old world luxury, the Hotel Ritz. At their head marched the imposing general of this one-man army, Ernest Hemingway, and his two volunteer aides, the distinguished Colonel David Bruce and "Moutarde," a prewar engineer on the French-owned Ethiopian railroads who had served as chief of staff of Hemingway's FFI army for the past four days.

In the Ritz's deserted lobby they found only one person, a frightened assistant manager. He recognized his distinguished American visitors, frequent pre-war guests at the hotel.

"Why," he gasped, "what are you doing here?"

They informed him they had come with some friends for a short stay. Recovering from his surprise, the assistant manager asked Hemingway if as a welcoming gesture there was anything the Ritz could offer him. The writer looked at his happy, scruffy horde of FFI already milling through the lobby.

"How about seventy-three dry martinis?" he answered.

Larry Collins and Dominique Lapierre,
Is Paris Burning?, p. 304

[Hemingway] was sitting with his "worthless characters" on the "nice delicate old furniture" in his room. They were field-stripping and cleaning weapons. Ernest had his boots off and was wearing "one of the two shirts" he owned. He was not prepared for the resplendent figure who came striding through the door. It was André Malraux in the uniform of a colonel, with gleaming cavalry boots.

"*Bonjour*, André," said Ernest.

"*Bonjour*, Ernest," Malraux replied. "How many have you commanded?"

Hemingway's answer was typically modest. "*Dix ou douze,*" said he, with studied insouciance. "*Au plus, deux cent.*"

Malraux's thin face contracted in the famous tic. "*Moi,*" he said, "*deux mille.*"

Hemingway fixed him with his coldest stare and said in level tones, "*Quel dommage* that we did not have the assistance of your force when we took this small town of Paris." Malraux's reply is not on record. But one of the partisans presently beckoned Ernest into the bathroom. "Papa," he whispered, "*on peut fusiller ce con?*" No, said Ernest, it would not be necessary to shoot the man. Offer him a drink and he would leave without bloodshed. So they offered him a drink and went on with their soldierly work in the sunny room, leaving their distinguished visitor to preen, jerk, and twitch until he rose to depart.

Carlos Baker, *Ernest Hemingway:
A Life Story,* pp. 419–20

Around the corner in the Ritz, another diner screamed in outrage. The waiter had just handed Ernest Hemingway the bill for his Liberation dinner.

"Millions to defend France," he declared, "thousands to honor your nation—but not one sou in tribute to Vichy." At the bottom of the check, the waiter had automatically included in the price of the meal the Vichy sales tax.

Larry Collins and Dominique Lapierre,
Is Paris Burning?, p. 326

He continued his entertaining on Saturday with a lunch at the Ritz for Helen Kirkpatrick, Ira Wolfert, John Reinhart, Charles Wertenbaker, and Irwin Shaw. Over the brandy Helen said that she and Reinhart were going to see the victory parade in its march towards Notre Dame. Ernest tried to argue her out of it. "Daughter," said he, "sit still and drink this good brandy. You can always watch parades but you'll never again celebrate the liberation of Paris at the Ritz."

Carlos Baker, *Ernest Hemingway: A Life Story*, p. 417

Another of Ernest's visitors at this time was a young, dark-haired sergeant in a CIC outfit. His name was Jerome D. Salinger and he was much impressed with his first sight of Hemingway.... He found Hemingway both friendly and generous, not at all impressed by his own eminence, and "soft"—as opposed to the hardness and toughness which some of his writing suggested. They got on very well, and Ernest volunteered to look at some of his work. Salinger returned to his unit in a state of mild exaltation.

Carlos Baker, *Ernest Hemingway: A Life Story*, p. 420

... he held court for a variety of visitors, including Jean-Paul Sartre, a short and voluble man in thick glasses, and Simone de Beauvoir. Sartre was curious about his opinion of William Faulkner. Ernest magnanimously admitted that Faulkner was a better writer than he. When Simone asked how ill Ernest really was, he kicked off the bedclothes and waved one muscular leg in her direction, "Healthy as hell," said he. For the moment, at least, he seemed to be on top of the world. But he later asserted that he had often "coughed the toilet at the Ritz full of blood." His brother Leicester, who occasionally dropped in, recalled the pallor of his face beneath the ragged beard, and the way he staggered back to bed after one of these bouts of retching, holding onto the furniture for support.

Carlos Baker, *Ernest Hemingway: A Life Story*, p. 439

Early in January [1945] he returned to the Ritz, taking up his former life as father-in-residence to officers and men of the 4th Infantry Division who came to Paris on leave. He later reported . . . that one of his visitors was the famous George Orwell, whom he had last seen in Barcelona. Orwell looked nervous and worried. He said that he feared that the Communists were out to kill him and asked Hemingway for the loan of a pistol. Ernest lent him the .32 Colt that Paul Willerts had given him in June. Orwell departed like a pale ghost.

Carlos Baker, *Ernest Hemingway: A Life Story*, pp. 441–42

His chief emotion was shame at having a rear-echelon address like the Hotel Ritz. He wanted nothing more than to rejoin his friends where the fighting was.

Carlos Baker, *Ernest Hemingway: A Life Story*, p. 430

I walked around to the Place Vendôme entrance of the Hôtel Ritz and asked the concierge, my acquaintance from 1940, if M. Hemingway was by chance in the hotel.

"Bien sûr," the concierge said, and directed me to Room 31. I rode up the coquettish little lift, the liftboy in his proper uniform and white gloves, knocked at No. 31, and asked the freckled soldier who opened the door if Mr. Hemingway was in.

"Papa, there's a dame here," Pfc. Archie Pelkey yelled into the room. Ernest emerged into the hallway, a whirlwind of good cheer, and gave me a welcoming merry-go-round bear hug, my feet succumbing to centrifugal force and nearly bashing in the walls. Inside the room a couple of his friends from the French underground, who had been with him since Rambouillet, were sitting on the bare floor intermittently cleaning rifles and sipping champagne.

Mary Welsh Hemingway, *How It Was*, pp. 109–10

The Ritz entrance on Place Vendôme.

The interior passage of the Ritz between rue Cambon and Place Vendôme.

In bed [at the Ritz] one quiet midnight he had asked, "Will you marry me, Pickle? Will you, Mary Welsh, take me, Ernest Hemingway for thy lawful wedded husband?"

I had demurred. "It's not orderly. I should settle, I should conclude my affairs with Noel first."

"They are really finished, aren't they, in your mind and your heart?"

"Yes."

"Then I'll marry us. You know I *mean* this?"

"Yes."

We would be faithful and true to each other, Ernest said. We would seek to understand and support each other in all times, troubles or triumphs. We would *never* lie to each other. We would love each other to the full extents of our capacities. I felt, drifting toward sleep, I could keep the promises—faithful, understanding, I hoped, not lying, loving. Ernest had been solemn.

Mary Welsh Hemingway,
How It Was, p. 126

Marlene [Dietrich] used to wander down to Ernest's room to sit on his bathtub and sing to him while he shaved, and they both generously forgave me when I mimicked her, especially her habit of approaching a note cautiously, wavering up and around it before she hit it solidly.

Mary Welsh Hemingway,
How It Was, p. 128

I walked through that lane of enchantment, the Ritz's passage from its Place Vendôme side to the rue Cambon, and after years of seeing drab London shop windows was more intoxicated by the gaiety and imagination of the stylish showcases along the walls than I had been by the champagne.

Mary Welsh Hemingway,
How It Was, p. 110

Ernest checked to see if Mary was in the hotel. She was not there and he "walked through the long alley where all the things were that you did not have the money to buy and admired them in their glass cases." Next to Mary, what he wanted most was a drink in the crowded bar on the rue Cambon side. . . .

Carlos Baker, *Ernest Hemingway:
A Life Story,* p. 429

His son Jack (nicknamed Bumby) had been wounded and captured on October 28 while Jack and another agent were reconnoitering at dusk inside enemy lines. . . . I could feel Ernest's temperature, blood pressure, anxiety, anger and frustration rising to some point of explosion with no safety valve apparent. . . .

. . . I hunted in my head for an escape from the misery. As Ernest was opening yet another bottle of champagne I suggested, "I'll bet you one hundred dollars I can make it from here to the Place du Tertre in ten minutes."

"With Sunday strollers, impossible."

"I know the short cuts." It would simply be too bad form for Ernest to get drunk, mourning his son's capture. But what else would he do, cooped up and ineffective in the Ritz? "From the rue Cambon door to the first step inside the Place. You'll have to time me, of course."

"One hundred, no odds?"

"Even money," I said, and we straightened our jackets, checked our watches and went along the many-splendored alley to the rue Cambon door. With Ernest trailing closely at first I walked, pushing through clusters of other walkers in the rue Halévy to the right of the Opéra, up the rue La Fayette, the rue Henri Monnier to the Boulevard Rochechouart, Ernest a hundred yards behind. Noticing my haste, a Parisian fell in beside me to ask, "Is he molesting you, mademoiselle, that large American soldier back there?"

"Non. Merci, monsieur. C'est une course."

I had less than two minutes to go when I reached the bottom of the long flight of the rue Foyatier steps and was running up them, dizzy and gasping, when Ernest yelled from below. I had lost my bet, but I had got Ernest exercising in fresh air. . . .

Ernest put himself to bed with apprehension as his companion that night, and the next morning awoke cheerful and with budding plans, as he did three hundred and sixty mornings a year in the seventeen years I shared with him.

Mary Welsh Hemingway,
How It Was, pp. 135–36

One of the first effects of the Liberation was the arrival of Hemingway at . . . [7] rue des Grands-Augustins. Pablo [Picasso] was still with Maya and her mother when he arrived. The concierge in Pablo's building was a very timid woman but not at all bashful. She had no idea who Hemingway was but she had been used to having many of Pablo's friends and admirers leave gifts for him when they called in his absence. From time to time South American friends of his had sent him such things as hams so that he could eat a little better than the average during the war. In fact Pablo had more than once shared food parcels with her. When she told Hemingway that Pablo was not there and Hemingway said he'd like to leave a message for him, she asked him—so she told us later—"Wouldn't you perhaps like to leave a gift for Monsieur?" Hemingway said he hadn't thought about it before but perhaps it was a good idea. He went out to his jeep and brought back a case of hand grenades. He set it down inside her *loge* and marked it "To Picasso from Hemingway."

Françoise Gilot and Carlton Lake,
Life with Picasso, p. 55

Rue Foyatier steps.

Another evening we went to the studio of M. Picasso . . . and M. Picasso was at home. He welcomed Ernest with open arms and while Picasso's girl, Françoise Gilot, a slim, dark, quiet girl with serpentine movements, and I kept ourselves behind them, Picasso showed Ernest the big, chilly studio and much of the work he had done in the past four years. *Les boches* left me alone," P.P. said. "They disliked my work, but they did not punish me for it." . . .

He showed us what seemed to be half a thousand canvases. . . . "There were some problems with the canvas and the paints, *tu sais,"* he said. He and Ernest were *tu-toi*-ing each other. "But I managed to resolve them."

The Paris sky was turning violet and Picasso took us to an open window overlooking the roofs and chimney pots on his level and just below. It was a tightly knit composition of lines and shapes, beautiful in tranquil colors. "There," said Picasso. "That is the best picture in my studio." He painted it at least once, I discovered later.

Mary Welsh Hemingway,
How It Was, p. 117

The American war correspondents were allocated the Hotel Scribe near the opera as their headquarters. Here they had their war room, public relations officers, censorship and transmission facilities. Hemingway did not appear. He was in trouble.

An army jealous of the regulations was on Hemingway's trail. It had been reported that contrary to international regulations . . . he, as a noncombatant, had taken an active part in the hostilities at Rambouillet. Charges had been laid against him. When the evidence was assembled he was to be tried by court-Martial.

Meanwhile he was living in some anxiety at the Ritz hotel. A curious combination this fellow. He had not the slightest fear of his own hide in the most dangerous type of warfare. . . .

One day a colonel of the judge advocate's department came into the Scribe bar and went from table to table where the correspondents were sitting. He was seeking evidence for the court-martial. He knew that in the later phase of the Rambouillet ac-

tion some of the other correspondents had been with Hemingway. He wanted them to testify that Hemingway had assembled the Resistance and that he had personally engaged in combat.

"Were you there?" he asked Kenneth Crawford.

"Oh, yes; I saw it all," Crawford answered.

"Will you testify at a court-martial?"

"Willingly."

"Would you mind telling me briefly what evidence you have?"

"I'll say it wasn't true. Ernie wasn't fighting. Have a drink, colonel."

The colonel looked pained and asked the same questions of others at the table. Braney McQuaid and I had not been at Rambouillet, but were perfectly willing to tell what we knew. Every man in the bar gave the same reply. The colonel worked for days and got nothing but frustration for his trouble. Any number of correspondents were willing to come forward, but not for the prosecution.

Marcel Wallenstein
"When Ernest Hemingway
Led Troops to Free France," p. 4c

[William Saroyan] was just outside the bar on the lower level of the Hôtel Scribe when he saw Hemingway in the midst of four or five war correspondents. One of them waved at Saroyan, who approached the group. "Here's Bill Saroyan," said his friend. "Where's Bill Saroyan?" said Ernest. Saroyan said, "In London you had a beard, but even without it I haven't forgotten you. Did shaving it off make you forget me?"

Carlos Baker, *Ernest Hemingway:
A Life Story,* p. 442

Group Captain Peter Wykeham Barnes of the RAF was on temporary leave in Paris, and happened to meet Ernest at the Scribe. "After taking in quite a quantity of grog," he wrote, "we adjourned to the George V for dinner. We went down to a lower floor to eat, and everything was ringing like bells when Ernest espied William Saroyan sitting two tables away. . . . This worked on him like a powerful injection. . . . He started by stating, 'Well, for God's sake, what's that lousy Armenian son of a bitch doing here?' The more . . . I tried to hush him, the worse it got. . . . Finally, Saroyan's companions . . . began to come back at Ernest. I'm not too sure how it developed, but shortly afterwards I was in a full-scale brawl, rolling about under the tables and banging the heads of total strangers on the wooden floors. I got the impression that someone bit my ankle. . . . The management arrived, reinforced I think by gendarmes, and the whole lot of us were thrown out *up* the stairs and into the Paris blackout. The two factions separated . . . Ernest was laughing like a hyena."

Carlos Baker, *Ernest Hemingway:*
A Life Story, p. 442

The little bar at the Ritz Hotel in Paris became a familiar haunt. Seldom empty, by noon it was so crowded one could scarcely be heard amid the chatter and the clinking of glasses. Bertin the bartender, spectacled and ruddy-faced, presided. Here we would rendez-vous before lunch or dinner, and here Ernest was sought out by old friends, acquaintances, or members of the press. Most of the characters who appear in *A Moveable Feast* were no longer in Paris; the people who came now were of a different era: Luis Quintanilla, the painter, a friend from the days of the Spanish Civil War; Juan Goytisolo, an angry young man of letters from Barcelona; Orson Welles, whom we had come across on our journey to Paris when we paused some three hours outside the city for a meal at a restaurant where the proprietor had greeted Ernest: "Oh, Mr. Welles, we are so happy to see you."

Valerie Danby-Smith,
"Reminiscence of Hemingway," p. 31

Many years later at the Ritz bar, long after the end of World War II, Georges, who is the bar chief now and who was the *chasseur* when Scott lived in Paris, asked me, "Papa, who was this Monsieur Fitzgerald that everyone asks me about?"

Hemingway, *A Moveable Feast,* p. 191

In 1959 [Hemingway and I] walked along the rue de Rivoli to number 224, and browsed among the books on the shelves of the Librairie Galignani. I see about me several books purchased on one of those occasions, selections prompted by Ernest: J. D. Salinger's *The Catcher in the Rye, The Man with the Golden Arm,* by Nelson Algren, John O'Hara's *From the Terrace,* the *Cantos* of Ezra Pound, and Lawrence Durrell's *Bitter Lemons.*

Valerie Danby-Smith,
"Reminiscence of Hemingway," p. 31

Far left: Interior of the rue Cambon Bar at the Ritz. *Center:* The restaurant at Hôtel George V. *Below:* Librairie Galignani.

One morning we walked down the rue de Castiglione and turned right towards the Place de la Concorde. There, across the street, is the Jeu de Paume, the little art gallery which houses the Impressionists, the same Manets, Monets, Cézannes that the young Hemingway went to see nearly every day at the Luxembourg museum. Ernest drew our attention to his favorites and, in particular, to one Cézanne that had influenced his early work. "I always try to write as good as the best picture that was ever painted," he said.

Valerie Danby-Smith,
"Reminiscence of Hemingway," p. 31

Below: Cézanne paintings in the Jeu de Paume museum.
Right: A door of the Jeu de Paume.

Bookstalls along the quais.

For we have been there in the books and out of the
books—and where we go, if we are any good, there
you can go as we have been.

Hemingway, *Green Hills of Africa,* p. 109

ACKNOWLEDGMENTS

Grateful acknowledgment is hereby made to the following publishers, agencies, and individuals for permission to reprint the material specified. All quotations from the works of Ernest Hemingway are fully protected by copyright and are used by permission.

The American Society of the French Legion of Honor, from "If He Hadn't Been a Genius He Would Have Been a Cad," by Alexander Winston. Copyright © 1972 by the *American Society Legion of Honor Magazine*.

The Boston Globe, from "Ernest Hemingway of Boston Put His Playfellows of Montparnasse into His Stories," by Joseph Hilton Smythe, published in *The Boston Sunday Globe*, December 18, 1927.

Denis Brian, from "The Importance of Knowing Ernest," by Denis Brian, first published in *Esquire* Magazine. Copyright © 1973 by Denis Brian.

Thomas Y. Crowell Company, Inc., from *The Expatriates*, by Ishbel Ross. Copyright © 1970 by Ishbel Ross.

Crown Publishers, Inc., from *Ernest Hemingway and the Little Magazines: The Paris Years*, by Nicholas Joost. Copyright © 1968 by Nicholas Joost.

The Delacorte Press, from *Exiles from Paradise: Zelda and Scott Fitzgerald*, by Sara Mayfield. Copyright © 1971 by Sara Mayfield.

Mrs. John Dos Passos, from *The Best Times: An Informal Memoir*, by John Dos Passos. Copyright © 1966 by John Dos Passos.

Doubleday & Company, Inc., from *We Were Interrupted*, by Burton Rascoe. Copyright © 1947 by Burton Rascoe.

Duke University Press, from *Expatriates and Patriots: American Artists, Scholars, and Writers In Europe*, by Ernest Earnest. Copyright © 1968 by Duke University Press. Durham, N.C.

Farrar, Straus & Giroux, Inc., from *The Apprenticeship of Ernest Hemingway*, by Charles A. Fenton, Copyright © 1954 by Charles A. Fenton.

————, from *Hemingway And His Critics: An International Anthology*, edited and with an Introduction by Carlos Baker. Copyright © 1961 by Hill and Wang (now a division of Farrar, Straus & Giroux, Inc.).

Harcourt Brace Jovanovich, Inc., from *The Heart to Artemis*, by Jackson Bryer. Copyright © 1962 by Norman Holmes Pearson.

————, from *Shakespeare and Company*, by Sylvia Beach. Copyright © 1956, 1959 by Sylvia Beach.

Harper & Row Publishers, Inc., from *A Late Education*, by Alan Moorehead. Copyright © 1970 by Alan Moorehead.

————, from *Back to Montparnasse*, by Sisley Huddleston. Copyright © 1931 by J. B. Lippincott Company. Copyright © renewed 1959 by Mrs. Sisley Huddleston.

Hawthorn Books, Inc., from *Hemingway: An Old Friend Remembers*, by Jed Kiley. Copyright © 1957 by Jed Kiley.

————, from *Paris Herald: The Incredible Newspaper*, by Al Laney. Copyright © 1947 by Al Laney.

Mary Hemingway and Alfred A. Knopf, Inc., from *How It Was*, by Mary Welsh Hemingway. Copyright © 1951, 1956, 1963, 1965, 1976 by Mary Welsh Hemingway.

David Higham Associates Limited, from *It Was the Nightingale*, by Ford Madox Ford.

Holt, Rinehart and Winston, from *Another Way of Living*, by John Bainbridge. Copyright © 1968 by John Bainbridge.

Hope Leresche & Sayle, from *My Friends When Young: The Memoirs of Brigit Patmore*, edited and with an introduction by Derek Patmore. Copyright © 1968 by Derek Patmore.

A. E. Hotchner and Random House, Inc., from *Papa Hemingway*, by A. E. Hotchner. Copyright © 1955, 1959, 1966 by A. E. Hotchner.

Houghton-Mifflin Company, from *A Continuing Journey*, by Archibald MacLeish. Copyright © 1967 by Archibald MacLeish; and, from *The Human Season: Selected Poems 1926–1972*, by Archibald MacLeish. Copyright © 1972 by Archibald MacLeish.

Information Handling Services, a division of Indian Head, Inc., and Matthew J. Bruccoli, from "The Sun Also Rose for Ernest Hemingway," by Victor Llona, reprinted from the *Fitzgerald/Hemingway Annual*, 1972, by Bruccoli/Clark Publishers. Copyright © 1973 by The National Cash Register Company.

Journal of Modern Literature, from "Hemingway's 'Fifty Grand': The Other Fight(s)," by James Martine. Copyright © 1971 by *Journal of Modern Literature*, Temple University.

The Kansas City Star, from "When Ernest Hemingway Led Troops to Free France," by Marcel Wallenstein. Copyright © 1949 by *The Kansas City Star*.

Alfred A. Knopf, Inc., and Mary Hemingway, from *How It Was*, by Mary Welsh Hemingway. Copyright © 1951, 1956, 1963, 1965, 1976, by Mary Welsh Hemingway.

BIBLIOGRAPHY

Anderson, Margaret. *My Thirty Years' War: An Autobiography by Margaret Anderson.* New York: Covici, Friede Publishers, 1930.

Bainbridge, John. *Another Way of Living.* New York: Holt, Rinehart and Winston, 1968.

Baker, Carlos. *Ernest Hemingway: A Life Story.* New York: Charles Scribner's Sons, 1969.

_____. *Hemingway and His Critics: An International Anthology.* Edited and with an Introduction by Carlos Baker. New York: Hill and Wang, 1961.

Bald, Wambly. "The Sweet Madness of Montparnasse." In *The Left Bank Revisited: Selections from the Paris Tribune 1917–1934*, edited and with an Introduction by Hugh Ford. University Park, Pa.: The Pennsylvania State University Press, 1972.

Beach, Sylvia. *Shakespeare and Company.* New York: Harcourt, Brace and Company, 1956.

Bishop, John Peale. "Homage to Hemingway." *The New Republic* 79 (November 11, 1936):39–42.

Bove, Charles F., with Dana Lee Thomas. *A Paris Surgeon's Story.* Boston: Little, Brown & Company, 1956.

Brian, Denis. "The Importance of Knowing Ernest." *Esquire* Magazine 77 (February 1972):98–101, 164–70.

Bryer, Jackson. *The Heart to Artemis.* New York: Harcourt, Brace and World, 1962.

Callaghan, Morley. *That Summer in Paris.* New York: Coward-McCann, Inc., 1963.

Collins, Larry, and Lapierre, Dominique. *Is Paris Burning?* New York: Simon and Schuster, Inc., 1965.

Cowley, Malcolm. *Exile's Return: A Literary Odyssey of the 1920's.* New York: The Viking Press, Compass Books, 1956.

_____. *A Second Flowering: Works and Days of the Lost Generation.* New York: The Viking Press, 1973.

Danby-Smith, Valerie. "Reminiscence of Hemingway." *Saturday Review* 47 (May 9, 1964):30–31, 57.

Dos Passos, John. *The Best Times: An Informal Memoir.* New York: The New American Library, 1966.

Earnest, Ernest. *Expatriates and Patriots: American Artists, Scholars, and Writers in Europe.* Durham, N.C.: Duke University Press, 1968.

Ellmann, Richard. *James Joyce.* New York: Oxford University Press, 1959.

Fenton, Charles A. *The Apprenticeship of Ernest Hemingway.* New York: The Viking Press, 1958.

Flanner, Janet. *Paris Was Yesterday.* New York: The Viking Press, 1968.

Franklin, Sidney. *The Bullfighter from Brooklyn.* Englewood Cliffs, N.J.: Prentice-Hall, Inc., 1952.

Gilot, Françoise, and Lake, Carlton. *Life with Picasso.* New York: The New American Library, Signet Books, 1965.

Glassco, John. *Memoirs of Montparnasse.* New York: The Viking Press, Compass Books, 1973.

Hemingway, Ernest. *Across the River and into the Trees.* New York: Charles Scribner's Sons, 1950.

_____. *By-Line: Ernest Hemingway.* Edited by William White. New York: Bantam Books, 1968.

_____. *The Collected Poems of Ernest Hemingway.* San Francisco: Pirated Edition, 1960.

_____. "French Politeness." *The Star Weekly,* Toronto, April 15, 1922.

_____. *Green Hills of Africa.* New York: Charles Scribner's Sons, 1935, 1963.

_____. *Islands in the Stream.* New York: Charles Scribner's Sons, 1970.

_____. *A Moveable Feast.* New York: Charles Scribner's Sons, 1964.

_____. "My Old Man." In *The Short Stories of Ernest Hemingway.* New York: Charles Scribner's Sons, 1938, 1966.

_____. "The Snows of Kilimanjaro." In *The Short Stories of Ernest Hemingway.* New York: Charles Scribner's Sons, 1938, 1966.

_____. *The Sun Also Rises.* New York: Charles Scribner's Sons, 1926, 1954.

_____. *The Torrents of Spring.* New York: Charles Scribner's Sons, 1972.

_____. "Wild Night Music of Paris Makes Visitor Feel a Man of the World." *The Star Weekly,* Toronto, March 25, 1922.

_____. *The Wild Years.* Edited by Gene Z. Hanrahan. New York: Dell Publishing Co., Inc., 1962.

Hemingway, Mary Welsh. *How It Was.* New York: Alfred A. Knopf, 1976.

_____. "Redbook Dialogue: Mary Hemingway and Robert Morley." *Redbook* 126 (November 1965): 62–63.

Hotchner, A. E. *Papa Hemingway.* New York: Random House, 1966.

Huddleston, Sisley. *Back to Montparnasse.* New York: J.B. Lippincott Company, 1931.

Joost, Nicholas. *Ernest Hemingway and the Little Magazines: The Paris Years.* Barre, Mass.: Barre Publishers, 1968.

Jordan, Philip. "Ernest Hemingway: A Personal Study."

Everyman: The World Weekly, December 12, 1929, p. 541.

Josephson, Matthew. *Life Among the Surrealists*. New York: Holt, Rinehart and Winston, 1962.

Kiley, Jed. *Hemingway: An Old Friend Remembers*. New York: Hawthorn Books, 1965.

Kuehl, John, and Bryer, Jackson, eds. *Dear Scott/Dear Max: The Fitzgerald-Perkins Correspondence*. New York: Charles Scribner's Sons, 1971.

Laney, Al. *Paris Herald: The Incredible Newspaper*. New York: D. Appleton-Century Company, Inc., 1947.

Llona, Victor. "The Sun Also Rose for Ernest Hemingway." In *Fitzgerald/Hemingway Annual*, 1972, edited by Matthew J. Bruccoli and C. E. Frazer Clark, Jr. Dayton, Ohio: NCR Microcard Editions, 1973.

MacLeish, Archibald. *A Continuing Journey*. Boston: Houghton Mifflin Company, 1968.

_____. *The Human Season: Selected Poems 1926–1972*. Boston: Houghton Mifflin Company, 1972.

Martine, James J. "Hemingway's 'Fifty Grand': The Other Fight(s)." *Journal of Modern Literature 2* (September 1971):123–27.

Mayfield, Sara. *Exiles from Paradise: Zelda and Scott Fitzgerald*. New York: Delacorte Press, 1971.

Moorehead, Alan. *A Late Education*. New York: Harper & Row, 1970.

Patmore, Brigit. *My Friends When Young: The Memoirs of Brigit Patmore*. Edited by Derek Patmore. London: William Heinemann, 1968.

Poli, Bernard J. *Ford Madox Ford and the Transatlantic Review*. Syracuse, N.Y.: Syracuse University Press, 1967.

Porter, Katherine Anne. "A Little Incident in the Rue de l'Odéon." *Ladies' Home Journal* 81 (August 1964):54–55.

Putnam, Samuel. *Paris Was Our Mistress: Memoirs of a Lost and Found Generation*. New York: The Viking Press, 1947.

Rascoe, Burton. *We Were Interrupted*. Garden City, N.Y.: Doubleday & Company, 1947.

Ray, Man. *Self Portrait*. Boston: Little Brown & Company, Atlantic Monthly Press Books, 1963.

Ross, Ishbel. *The Expatriates*. New York: Thomas Y. Crowell Company, 1970.

Samuels, Lee, ed. *A Hemingway Check List*. New York: Charles Scribner's Sons, 1951.

Smythe, Joseph Hilton. "Ernest Hemingway of Boston Put His Playfellows of Montparnasse into His Stories." *The Sunday Boston Globe*, December 18, 1927, p. 3.

Sokoloff, Alice Hunt. *Hadley: The First Mrs. Hemingway*. New York: Dodd, Mead & Company, 1973.

Stein, Gertrude. *The Autobiography of Alice B. Toklas*. New York: Random House, Vintage Books, 1960.

Stock, Noel. *The Life of Ezra Pound*. New York: Random House, Pantheon Books, 1970.

Turnbull, Andrew. *Scott Fitzgerald*. New York: Charles Scribner's Sons, 1962.

Wallenstein, Marcel. "When Ernest Hemingway Led Troops to Free France." *The Kansas City Star*, Sunday, September 4, 1949, pp. 1c, 4c.

Wickes, George. *Americans in Paris*. Garden City, N.Y.: Doubleday & Company, Inc., Paris Review Editions, 1969.

Williams, William Carlos. *The Autobiography of William Carlos Williams*. New York: Random House, 1951.

Winston, Alexander. "If He Hadn't Been a Genius He Would Have Been a Cad." *American Society Legion of Honor Magazine* 3, No. 1 (1972):25–40.

PICTURE CREDITS

INDEX

Numbers in *italics* indicate photographs of the subject mentioned.